ST PAUL'S CATHEDRAL

ST PAUL'S CATHEDRAL

1400 YEARS AT THE HEART OF LONDON

Ann Saunders

SCALA

CONTENTS

CLARENCE HOUSE

St. Paul's Cathedral is Sir Christopher Wren's great masterpiece and, with all its historical - and contemporary - associations with the City of London and with our national life, is rightly known throughout the world as one of the great international symbols of our Christian faith. Its incomparable architecture speaks of the majesty of God and of the mysteries of faith.

There has, however, been a need over many years for a study of St. Paul's which tells something of the history of this great building and its site: of the earlier cathedrals that stood at the top of Ludgate Hill; of the Great Fire of London; of the appointment of Sir Christopher Wren and his lifetime's work in building the Cathedral. But there are also the monuments and the memorials; the great occasions over three hundred years which have brought the nation to worship beneath the Dome of St. Paul's; the trauma of the Second World War; the continuing responsibility of successive Deans and Chapters in caring for the building and the concern today to ensure that St. Paul's remains a centre of Christian worship and mission.

Dr Ann Saunders introduces her book by saying that, "It takes time to get to know St. Paul's". I hope that her telling of this marvellous story will make it possible for large numbers of people to come to know the Cathedral that lies at the heart of London and - in so many ways - at the heart of our nation.

I commend this account of the story of St. Paul's and hope it will bring pleasure, and greater understanding, to everyone who reads it.

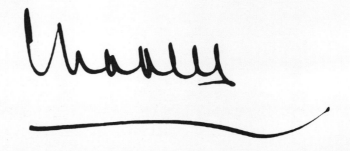

INTRODUCTION

O N A SMALL HILL in the western part of the City of London stands St Paul's Cathedral. Today's building is not the first to occupy the site, for this has been a place of Christian worship for 1,400 years. The medieval Cathedral, with a tower and spire soaring above the city, was at the time one of the wonders of Europe.

Sir Christopher Wren's St Paul's, built after the Fire of London of 1666, has become the City's most familiar landmark, its dome with the ball and cross above it symbolic of London's steadfastness down the centuries and its endurance throughout the bombing of the Second World War. We know the building so well that we take it for granted, giving it no more than an affectionate upward glance as we hurry through the churchyard or up Ludgate Hill. But when it was newly completed, in the early eighteenth century, it was awe-inspiring, breathtaking, unlike any other cathedral or church built in Britain, an immense space to be comprehended – or at least accepted – in its entirety.

It is an austere space, dignified and solemn; though there are few intimate corners, it is not unfriendly; it is always uplifting. St Paul's is a place of worship designed by a deeply religious man, reared in the Church of England, who was by nature and training a mathematician. Unlike other cathedrals and major places of worship in Britain, St Paul's did not grow organically, adding an aisle or a chapel as needed. It was planned from the beginning, its immense space expressing the universal but abstract nature of God and religion. For 1,400 years, London and Londoners have registered their joys and sorrows, their hopes and fears, even their strong social and political views, in or around St Paul's. The Cathedral is still the place to which they come in times of emergency or unexpected delight. All who come have been welcomed and, according to their need, have received advice or comfort freely given. It takes time to get to know St Paul's.

This book has been written in the hope that – in telling the story of the centuries of prayer offered on this hilltop, of the building of the present Cathedral and of its subsequent history – visitors and Londoners alike may be helped to look at St Paul's with a new and joyful wonder.

Fig. 1 South portico of St Paul's under snow. This photograph was taken from the Millennium Bridge so that the buildings on the south side of St Paul's Churchyard seem to crowd in on the Cathedral.

1

THE MEDIEVAL CATHEDRAL

THE FIRST ST PAUL'S WAS BUILT in the seventh century by Mellitus, one of the monks who came to Britain with St Augustine. Pope Gregory the Great had sent Augustine from Rome as a missionary in AD 597. Christianity was known in these northern isles in the second century, but after the withdrawal of the Romans in 410 it had been in decline. The Pope hoped to draw the people back into the Church of Rome.

The two main cities in Roman times had been London and York, and Pope Gregory instructed Augustine to establish archbishoprics in those places. Augustine landed on the south coast of Britain, where his little band, which included Mellitus, was welcomed by Bertha, the Frankish Christian princess married to Ethelbert, King of Kent. Ethelbert was converted to Christianity by Augustine at Canterbury, and afterwards Augustine remained there; thus it was that Canterbury became the seat of the archbishopric.

Mellitus was consecrated bishop by Augustine. He left Canterbury and reached London in 604, establishing there a cathedral dedicated to St Paul. Mellitus came at a strange time, for the Anglo-Saxon population had moved westwards, up the River Thames, leaving the Roman city half-abandoned. After Ethelbert's death the south of England returned to paganism (fig. 2), though repeated attempts were made to re-establish Christianity. In 668 Theodore became Archbishop of Canterbury, and in 675 he consecrated Erkenwald Bishop of London. Erkenwald was canonised after his death, and his shrine in St Paul's drew pilgrims from all over Europe.

No one knows what the first building looked like. It may well have been of wood, though it might have been easier to build a place of worship from the broken pieces of Roman stone and brick and tile that were to hand. A little church of this type was built by Cedd, a missionary from Northumbria, at Bradwell-on-Sea in Essex where he landed on his journey southwards; it stands to this day, lonely amid the marshes.

St Paul's was destroyed by fire in 675 and by the Danes in 961; each time, St Erkenwald's body was saved and restored to a shrine in the rebuilt Cathedral. The tenth-century building was of stone. This too went when a terrible conflagration swept through the London of the Normans in 1087.

The bishop at that time was Maurice, who had been William the Conqueror's chaplain. A man of resolve, he began the rebuilding and the creation of what was to become one of the largest and most imposing buildings in Europe. Work extended over almost a hundred years; the choir was completed in 1148, the nave, twelve bays long with soaring Romanesque arches, by 1200, and the tower, 245 feet (75 m) high, by 1221. Between 1258 and 1314 the choir and chancel were rebuilt, the expansion necessitating the demolition of the parish church of St

Fig. 2 Anglo-Scandinavian grave-marker, second quarter of the eleventh century. The Runic inscription reads, 'Ginna and Toki had this stone laid'; it does not tell us who was commemorated. Presumably set in a wall, it was found just inside the southern boundary of St Paul's Churchyard.

Fig. 3 St Paul's around 1250 from *Historia Anglorum* by Matthew Paris. The illustration shows London from the north, encircled by walls. The loftiness of the spire made the Cathedral one of the wonders of European architecture.

Faith at the east end (fig. 4). Parishioners were given the right to worship in the crypt where there is, even now, a chapel dedicated to St Faith. The final addition to the structure was the chapter house, which lay to the south-west of St Paul's. It was built in the mid-fourteenth century, to the designs of William of Ramsey.

The medieval Cathedral was enormous, a source of great pride to Londoners. Its overall length was 585 feet (178 m), and its transepts extended for 290 feet (88 m); it was the longest church in England, considerably longer and broader than the present Cathedral (fig. 3). The tower was topped by a spire, one of the loftiest in Europe, reaching 489 feet (149 m) into the air; today the cross above the dome of St Paul's is just 365 feet (111 m) above the Cathedral floor. Twice, in 1341 and 1444, the spire was struck by lightning; each time it was reconstructed. The earliest spire was surmounted by a ball and cross, the later ones with weathercocks. The spire was the Cathedral's most notable feature. On the stone of the wall inside the bell-tower of St Mary's Church at Ashwell in Hertfordshire is a scratched drawing of St Paul's: in the Middle Ages a villager must have visited London, marvelled at the spire and returned home to record what he had seen.

The transepts were a useful short cut to and from the buildings to north and south of the Cathedral. The clergy struggled against this. At intervals, injunctions were brought in forbidding trade within the church, the carrying of burdens, ball games and all sorts of sports, but with little success. The Cathedral *was* London, and Londoners loved it, treating it with the familiarity reserved for that which is most dear. They were proud of the Cathedral; it was *their*

Cathedral, unlike Westminster Abbey, which was the king's place. The only two royal tombs dated from before the Norman Conquest: those of Sebba, who had endowed St Paul's with the Manor of Tillingham in Essex, and Ethelred the Unready. The Cathedral had been built not by extraordinary royal expenditure but by the devotion of the clergy and the steady charity of all manner of people, low as well as high. And if the Abbey had Edward the Confessor's body, St Paul's cherished St Erkenwald's.

In the north-eastern corner of the precinct stood St Paul's Cross, an outdoor pulpit from which the doctrines of the faith were preached by 1241. To some extent the Cathedral benefited from the religious upheaval, as a result of which Henry VIII made himself head of the Church of England. Properties that had belonged to Westminster Abbey were made over to it – 'robbing Peter to pay Paul', men said. But the four Jesus bells that hung in the separate bell-tower were cut down and gambled away by Henry VIII to Sir Miles Partridge, who sold them off as scrap metal; Partridge, accused of treason in the succeeding reign, was beheaded

ECCLESIÆ PAROCHIALIS S. FIDIS
PROSPECTVS INTERIOR.

Quo cum amplius non erit, quale olim fuerit, notum sit, Descriptorem egit
GVIL: BISHOP Arm.
At quanta supersunt quæ videt ipsa fides.

FIDEM HÆC EXHIBET, ILLA DEVM.

W. Hollar delin. et sculp.

on Tower Hill. Worse still, the shrine of St Erkenwald was despoiled of its gold and jewels.

The slow decline of the medieval Cathedral was beginning. Elizabeth succeeded to the throne in November 1558, and from then on St Paul's became a reformed Cathedral. Three years later the spire burned down for the third time; it was never replaced. The casual use of the interior – as a meeting-place, as a market-place, as a thoroughfare – continued undiminished; Ben Jonson set a scene of his play *Every Man Out of His Humour* there. Although a service of thanksgiving was held in St Paul's in 1588 to celebrate the defeat of the Spanish Armada, by the end of Elizabeth's long reign cracks were appearing in the masonry and the roof was leaking. Nobody did anything except patch up the worst areas; the task seemed too great.

In 1603 James I came to the throne, and one Londoner was stirred into action. His name was Henry Farley, and he was a member of the Scriveners' Company. In 1615 he began to petition the Lord Mayor, to write and publish tracts and poems about the state of the Cathedral and to send letters to the King. He commissioned from the artist John Gipkyn two huge painted panels of St Paul's as it was and as he felt it should be (figs 7 and 8). In an inscription the building entreats the monarch:

View oh Kinge how my wall creepers
Have made me worke for chimney sweepers

Fig. 5 Twelfth-century psalter, recorded in the inventory of the treasury of St Paul's, 1486. The saints commemorated and the donors remembered in prayers have strong Cathedral connections. The volume is 33.5 x 22 cm (13¼ x 8¾ in.).

In the right-hand panel of the diptych a crowd is gathered in St Paul's Churchyard, listening to the preacher. A dog barks and is chased away by a man with a stick. A two-storey building has been erected against the Cathedral; in the upper tier sit King James, Queen Anne and Prince Charles, with members of the Court beside them; below are the Lord Mayor and Aldermen. Houses with smoking chimneys have been built against the adjacent wall. The left-hand painting shows St Paul's as Farley longed to see it, restored and with a new, more modest spire rebuilt. Angels pour their blessings from the skies.

At one point Farley was so importunate that he was imprisoned in Ludgate, but in the end, on 26 March 1620, James I came to St Paul's and heard a sermon about the need for repairs; he declared he would live on bread and water in order to further the work, and promised £2,000. Stone began to be brought in, some of which George Villiers, Duke of Buckingham, appropriated to build the York Watergate, which exists still beside the Thames. But though John Donne, the great preacher and poet, had become Dean of the Cathedral in 1621, little happened to put the building to rights (fig. 9).

It was not until 1631 – by which time Charles I was on the throne, eager to see his capital enhanced, and William Laud was Bishop of London – that a start was made on the work. The King's own Surveyor, Inigo Jones (fig. 10), was put in charge of both the design and the

Fig. 6 A cathedral choir, ranged in order of size and pitch of voice, would gather round an antiphonal to read the words and music. This fifteenth-century Italian example was acquired by St Paul's Library in 1894. It measures 51.5 x 35.6 cm (20¼ x 14 in.).

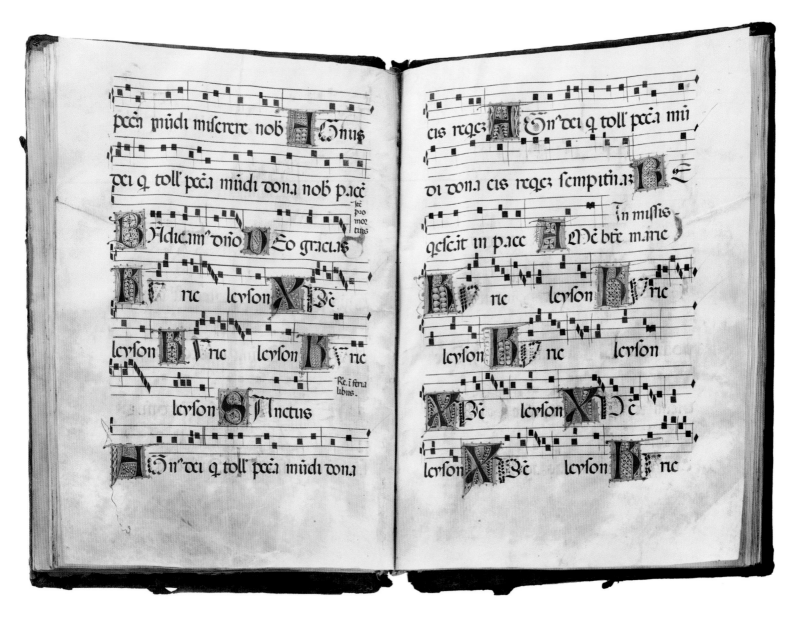

Fig. 7 Diptych was commissioned by Henry Farley from John Gipkyn, a deaf and dumb member of the Painter Stainers' Company. The left-hand panel shows St Paul's as Farley longed to see it, with a new spire adorned with golden statues of the royal family and angels circling round it in the skies.

Fig. 8 The right-hand panel shows the Cathedral as it really was – dirty, with houses built up against it, shorn of its spire and sinister black birds flying round the stump of the tower. James, his Queen and Prince Charles sit in a gallery, listening to an open-air sermon; a dog barks and is whipped away.

operation. Beginning at the east end, the vast medieval building was encased in Portland stone, while to the west end was added a gigantic Corinthian portico. However strange this may now seem, contemporary eyes saw no incongruity. John Webb, Inigo Jones's pupil and successor, declared that the portico 'contracted the envy of all Christendom upon our Nation, for a Piece of Architecture not to be parallel'd in these last ages of the World' (fig. 11). Charles I took upon himself the sole responsibility for its cost; the final outlay on the work was £101,330 4s. 8d.

By the late summer of 1642 the scaffolding was in place for the restoration of the tower and the interior. It was never put to use; war had broken out between King and Parliament, the timber was sold off to provide arrears of pay to the Parliamentary army, and the great building was turned into a cavalry barracks – at one point 800 horses were stabled there. Booths and shops were built against the portico; the colonnade which had been a source of pride to king, bishop and architect became a place for sordid hucksters.

Many must have been horrified at what was happening; one man had the courage to act. That man was Sir William Dugdale, who employed the artist William Sedgwick to draw both St Paul's Cathedral and Westminster Abbey, and to copy out all the monumental inscriptions. The drawings were engraved by the Bohemian artist Wenceslaus Hollar, who had made his home in England. Dugdale, who had fought for the King, spent the Commonwealth period writing a history of St Paul's.

When in 1660 Charles II was restored to the throne, the great church was a wreck. The Bishop of London, Gilbert Sheldon, and the new Dean, William Sancroft, turned to a young man of science, Christopher Wren, for advice on how the Cathedral might be put in order.

Fig. 9 The monument to John Donne, poet and Dean of St Paul's, was the only complete sculpture to survive the Fire. A painting was done of him wrapped in his shroud, and from this Nicholas Stone carved the memorial.

Fig. 10 Inigo Jones undertook the restoration of the Cathedral in the 1630s. Having travelled to Italy, he brought the ideals of classical architecture to England. He laid out Covent Garden, the first example of real town-planning in England.

OPPOSITE:
Fig. 11 The portico Inigo Jones added to the west end, 1633–42. Daniel King's elevation, published 1718.

IGNATII IONES MAG: BRIT: ARCHITECTI GE-
NERALIS VERA EFFIGIES,

Anth: van Dyck Eques pinxit.   W: Hollar fecit, aqua forti.

2
CHRISTOPHER WREN

CHRISTOPHER WREN'S extraordinary abilities were recognised from childhood. Born on 20 October 1632 at East Knoyle, in Wiltshire, he was the only son to survive of the Revd Dr Christopher Wren and his wife, Mary. He was a delicate child but not a lonely one, for there were daughters. Susanna, the second one and five years his elder, was Christopher's particular friend and supporter, and was to have a great, if largely unacknowledged, influence on his life.

The Revd Dr Wren had an older brother, Matthew. As boys, both attended Merchant Taylors' School in the City of London, where their quickness and intelligence caught the attention of Lancelot Andrewes, then Dean of Westminster, when he came to the school to make the annual inspection. Andrewes obtained for Matthew a scholarship to Pembroke College, Cambridge, where he himself was Master; after the young man took holy orders, he became Andrewes's chaplain. Matthew Wren went on to become Master of Peterhouse, Cambridge, then Dean of Windsor and Registrar of the Most Noble Order of the Garter, and finally, in succession, Bishop of Hereford, Norwich and Ely. His nephew Christopher would perhaps have visited him at Ely and known the cathedral in the flat fen country; the breadth of its central crossing and the way the light filters into it through an octagon may have been remembered all his life, echoing throughout his mature achievements.

While he was Rector of East Knoyle, the Revd Dr Wren, the architect's father, gave the church a strong new roof and adorned the chancel with biblical scenes executed in lively plasterwork. He succeeded his brother as Dean of Windsor, and it was in that pleasant town, close to the royal castle, that his son, Christopher, spent his early years.

Christopher was a precocious child, his hands as dextrous as his mind was quick, and he was sweet-tempered, patient and steady. After being taught at home by a tutor, Dr Shepheard, until the age of ten, he was sent to Westminster School. From there, in a child's unformed hand, he wrote a long, affectionate letter to his father in Latin, promising that he would always try to do his best; it seems probable that by this time his mother was already dead.

What is known of Sir Christopher's early years comes from a manuscript account entitled *Parentalia*, compiled by his son, another Christopher. Into this he put everything that he could remember or find out about his father; the manuscript was published by *his* son, Stephen Wren, Doctor of Medicine, in 1750.

In the summer of 1642 war broke out between King Charles I and his Parliament. Windsor Castle fell into Parliamentarian hands, and Dr Wren was turned out of his deanery. He and his family went to stay with his daughter Susanna, who at the age of sixteen had married William Holder, Rector of Bletchingdon in Oxfordshire. Besides being a clergyman,

Fig. 12 The young Christopher Wren, sculpted by Edward Pierce. This is a copy of perhaps the finest seventeenth-century English portrait bust. Pierce also worked as a carver at St Paul's.

Dr Holder was an excellent mathematician, and he soon noticed and encouraged Christopher's own remarkable aptitude.

In 1649, with the support of his family and tutors, Christopher Wren went up to Wadham College, Oxford. In a time so troubled politically, some turned with double zeal to intellectual pursuits. Wren began to attend the weekly meetings of an informal group of men attached to or visiting the university who were interested in natural philosophy and the emerging sciences. Religion and politics were avoided; the discussion was, as one of the company, Dr John Willis, wrote:

> of philosophical enquiries, and such as related thereunto: as physick, anatomy, geometry, astronomy, navigation, staticks, magneticks, chymicks, mechanicks, and natural experiments with the state of those studies as then calculated at home and abroad.

It was this 'new learning' that excited these men's minds.

From these gatherings Wren learned much and made many friends who were to be of help to him in later life; his intelligence was such that he was recognised as an equal by those twice or three times his age. He invented an instrument for writing in the dark, and a pen for producing simultaneously two separate copies of a document. There were experiments with telescopes and sundials, and Wren made a model of the visible side of the moon.

In the autumn of 1653 Wren, then just twenty-one, was elected a Fellow of All Souls. Soon after being admitted to the fellowship, Wren made the acquaintance of John Evelyn, who wrote in his diary (13 July 1654) of meeting 'that miracle of a youth, Mr Christopher Wren'. Two days later Evelyn dined with Dr Williams, the Principal of Wadham College; Wren was of course present and gave Evelyn a piece of white marble 'which he had stained with a lively red, very deepe, as beautiful as if it had been natural'. This was presumably for Evelyn's cabinet of curiosities. The friendship between Wren and Evelyn ended only with the latter's death in 1706 (fig. 13).

In 1657 Wren was appointed Professor of Astronomy at Gresham College in London. The college had been established sixty years earlier, under the will of the great Elizabethan financier Sir Thomas Gresham. Seven professors lectured in the great hall of what had been Sir Thomas's own home, chiefly on the new sciences that were changing men's outlook on the world. What was extraordinary was that the lectures were given in both English and Latin, and admission to them was free. Wren took up this new work with enthusiasm, and the men who had met together in Oxford attended the London lectures and continued the discussion. It was from these meetings that the Royal Society, England's premier scientific body, was to develop.

Oliver Cromwell died on 3 September 1658, and after nearly two years of political vacillation the throne was offered to the exiled son of the dead king; he returned to England in May 1660 to be crowned Charles II. He too was fascinated by the sciences; he had a telescope set up, and he commissioned Wren to construct for him a lunar globe, which the young scholar did with great success. The two men were almost the same age – the King was thirty, Wren was twenty-eight – and they had serious interests in common.

In 1661 Wren was appointed Savilian Professor of Astronomy at Oxford. He resigned the Gresham professorship but continued to spend much time in London. The King was anxious for him to go to Tangiers, to supervise the construction of fortifications there, and it is known from contemporary correspondence that Wren was already being consulted about St Paul's. He refused the Tangiers appointment on account of the delicacy of his health, and must have begun to think about the ancient, battered Cathedral and how it could best be restored.

Chance, and his university connections, had already turned his mind to architecture. His uncle, Bishop Matthew Wren, imprisoned in the Tower of London by the Parliamentarians, was released at last from captivity after Charles's return. He longed as a thanksgiving to build

Fig. 13 John Evelyn, diarist, virtuoso, diplomat, courtier, gardener, man of letters and of science, and Wren's lifelong friend. This portrait, by Hendryck van der Borcht the younger, was painted c. 1641.

a chapel for his old Cambridge college, Pembroke, and asked his nephew to undertake the work; the results were exquisite. At the same time Gilbert Sheldon, who too had suffered under Cromwell and had been ejected as Warden of All Souls, was made Bishop of London. He decided to give Oxford a handsome gift; what it needed was a building for academic ceremonial, and Wren was commissioned to construct the Sheldonian Theatre.

It must have been at this point that Wren realised where his skills should be directed. Architecture was mathematics made solid, music made visible, and he began to read and

Fig. 14 Jean Marot's engraving of the main façade of the new Sorbonne University buildings. The Sorbonne was founded in 1257 by Robert de Sorbonne, but Jacques Lemercier was commissioned to build afresh and created the elegant domed church, which Wren must have seen.

study every available book and to collect engravings, drawings and ground-plans of buildings. Term having ended, he went in June 1665 to Paris, where great works were in hand. This was fortunate, for that summer plague raged in London and spread throughout the country.

For a man intent upon architecture, Paris was at that moment the most exciting city in Europe. It was true that, at last – after 120 years of work and planning, by thirteen architects during the reigns of twenty popes – St Peter's in Rome was complete with its great dome, while the middle years of the century saw Giovanni Lorenzo Bernini's glorious laying-out of the piazza before the majestic building. But France had a young and ambitious king, Louis XIV, served by a great and far-seeing minister, Jean-Baptiste Colbert. After bitter civil wars Colbert was resolved on concentrating all power in royal hands and a central government, in Paris: Versailles was, as yet, little more than a hunting-lodge. In 1665 the Palais du Louvre was being enlarged and the Tuileries palace reconstructed, while all around them the capital was being rebuilt in stone, its streets paved and its riverside embanked. The Sorbonne had its dome (fig. 14), as had the churches of Val-del-Grâce and the Visitation, and the convent of St Anne-la-Royale. The most creative architects of France and Italy were all in Paris – Louis Le Vau, Jacques Lemercier, François Mansart and Guarino Guarini – each striving to outdo the others, and they were joined in 1665 by Bernini himself, his piazza in Rome having been completed a few years before.

Wren probably met them all; even Bernini, grudgingly, gave the young man a moment's glance at his secret plans (which were never to be realised) for the east façade of the Louvre. But what impressed the Englishman most were the scale of the undertaking and the orderliness of it all – the masses of stone that went into the making of the quays, and the regularity with which the workmen were paid each Sunday.

While he was in Paris, Wren met the leading French scientists of the day. In the one letter that survives from the expedition, written to an unknown friend whom we may guess to have been John Evelyn, he lists fourteen châteaux that he visited and tells of his travels around the Parisian countryside. He returned to England in the spring of 1666 and resumed his lectures at Oxford. The need for restoration at St Paul's was a matter of common discussion.

On 1 May 1666 Wren presented a report, with drawings, to the Royal Commission on St Paul's (figs 15 and 16). In the report he argued against either an attempt at 'too great Magnificence' in the restoration or a mere patch-up, and recommended a middle course. He observed that the great pillars, some 11 feet (3.6 m) thick, which supported the ruined tower, were leaning 6 inches (15 cm) out of alignment, and suggested lightening the load by replacing the tower with a spacious dome or 'Rotundo, with a Cupola, or hemispherical Roof, and upon the Cupola, (for the outward Ornament) a Lantern with a Spiring Top'.

A meeting was held in the old Cathedral on 27 August 1666. Among those present, besides Gilbert Sheldon, Archbishop of Canterbury, and William Sancroft, Dean of St Paul's, were the skilful amateur architect Sir Roger Pratt, Hugh May of the Royal Office of Works, 'several expert workmen' and the diarist John Evelyn, who had been appointed one of the Commissioners. Evelyn's diary entry makes it clear that there was fierce and prolonged argument but that finally Wren's proposal, which Evelyn supported, prevailed:

We had a mind to build it with a noble cupola, a forme of church-building not as yet known in England, but of wonderfull grace: for his purpose we offer'd to bring in a plan and estimate, which, after much contest, was at last assented to.

The gathering broke up; Evelyn – and possibly Wren – 'went with my Lord Bishop to the Deans's'. Six days later Evelyn wrote:

2 Sept. This fatal night about ten, began that deplorable fire neere Fish Streete in London.

Fig. 15 Wren was originally asked to design improvements to the existing building. This pre-Fire design shows Wren's early essay in replacing the tower with a dome.

Fig. 16 The cross-section, from west to east, shows Wren's Gothic and classical alternatives for the vaulting – Gothic on the right, classical on the left.

3

THE GREAT FIRE OF LONDON

THE GREAT FIRE, which destroyed four-fifths of medieval London, broke out in the small hours of Sunday, 2 September 1666. It started in a baker's shop in Pudding Lane, near the north end of London Bridge. Afterwards, Thomas Farynor, the king's baker, swore that he had put out his fire by ten o'clock on Saturday night and that, when he needed a candle at midnight, there was no spark among the embers and that he had had to go elsewhere for a light. Whatever the truth, in the early hours of the morning the brushwood and faggots beside the oven caught fire.

Farynor's assistant was awoken by the smoke; he roused the family, and they scrambled out on to the roof and, with the aid of a gutter, reached the house next door in safety. A poor maidservant, not daring to attempt the passage, died in the flames. Witnesses were later to say that Farynor's house burned for a full hour before the fire spread; the next-door neighbour was able to get his household goods to safety.

Few people were around so early, and there was no one to give a general warning or take official action. The Lord Mayor, Sir Thomas Bludworth, was roused at about three in the morning but dismissed the matter: 'Pish! a woman might piss it out', he is reported to have said. Samuel Pepys, from whose diary we know so much of Restoration London, looked out of his window at the same time: 'I thought it far enough off, and so went to bed and to sleep', he wrote.

The weather played a part in events. It had been a parched summer, and by September the houses of London, built chiefly of timber, lath and plaster, many of them with thatched roofs, were tinder-dry. In the clear autumn morning a wind was blowing steadily from the north-east. Once the fire had taken hold, sparks were wafted into the yard of the Star Inn on Fish Street Hill, where straw and hay and other combustibles were lying. The blaze spread to Thames Street, into the lanes running down to the river and so to the wharves and storage warehouses along the waterside. Here were supplies of oil, coal, timber, hemp, tallow and tar; the resulting conflagration spread to the north end of London Bridge, beside which was the Thames Water House, with pumps that could raise supplies from the river. It was quickly destroyed; London was bereft of mechanical firefighting aids; the only equipment was hand-held syringes and billhooks to pull down the thatched roofs.

By this time it was daylight, and the Lord Mayor was properly aware of the danger. One course was open to him – to isolate and so starve the fire by pulling down or blowing up the houses in its path – but he hesitated to cause so much damage and incur so much expense. Steadily the fire spread inland, with the curve of the river assuming the shape of a drawn bow; the preacher Thomas Vincent described it as 'a bow which had God's arrow in it with a flaming point'.

OVERLEAF:
Fig. 19 A contemporary representation of the Fire by a Dutch artist, possibly developed from sketches made by an eye-witness. The Tower of London remains intact and London Bridge comparatively unscathed, but the flames are about to engulf the medieval Cathedral.

Etiam periere Ruinæ

W. Hollar fecit A° 1666

Fig. 17 Flames and smoke belch from the Cathedral in this small contemporary engraving. It was used as the title-page to a seventeenth-century sermon.

Fig. 18 A drawing by Thomas Wyck of the ruins of St Paul's, *c.* 1673. Workmen stand perilously on top of a remnant of the south transept; Samuel Pepys felt sick at the sight of the great stones falling.

King Charles, alerted by Pepys, came to view the situation and instructed Lord Craven, the popular son of a former Lord Mayor, to do all he could to assist the City authorities. Night fell; the fire ate its way northwards. By Monday it had reached Cornhill and consumed the Royal Exchange. The streets were thronged with people trying to save their goods; the price of a cart and horse rose by the hour. Some organised attempt was made to get matters under control – eight firefighting posts, each manned by 130 citizens and soldiers, were set up around the City – but the flames had taken too strong a grasp, and the wind continued to blow relentlessly.

By Tuesday the conflagration was widespread. The flames took hold of the Guildhall so that it stood, as Vincent said, 'in a bright, shining coal, as if it had been a palace of gold, or a great building of burnished brass'. They then pushed westwards and reached St Paul's Cathedral. (figs 17 and 19)

The Churchyard afforded an open space around the great building, so it was judged – understandably – that the flames would spare it. Stationers and booksellers, whose shops stood around the Churchyard, evacuated their stock to St Faith's Chapel, in the crypt, believing that there, at least, their goods would be safe. They were wrong. At about eight o'clock in the evening a firebrand, carried overhead by the wind, fell on the roof of the Cathedral, where boards had been laid to cover broken leadwork. The timber above the stone vaulting broke into such a blaze that William Taswell, a Westminster School boy, standing a mile away, could easily read the diminutive print of a tiny pocket edition of Terence that he had with him. The lead roof melted and flowed in torrents down Ludgate Hill.

Meanwhile, shop goods – and in particular the bolts of cloth from nearby drapery stores, piled up against the Cathedral walls when there was no more time or space to cram them into the crypt or within the doors – led the flames up to St Paul's. Inigo Jones's Portland stone refacing shattered away from the underlying structure – 'the stones of St Paul's flew like granados [grenades]', John Evelyn wrote. The monuments to the dead within the Cathedral – to John of Gaunt, Duke of Lancaster, and his wife, Blanche, whose death Chaucer had lamented, to Elizabeth's courtiers, Sir Christopher Hatton, Sir Francis Walsingham and his son-in-law the heroic Sir Philip Sidney – were all destroyed. The charred remnants of an armoured figure, from Sir Nicholas Bacon's memorial, remained; he was the father of the more famous Sir Francis Bacon. One effigy alone survived intact: that of the poet–dean John Donne. (fig. 9)

By this time the King, his brother James, Duke of York, and the City authorities were making effective efforts to bring the flames under control. Towards evening on Wednesday the wind dropped, and, though the destruction reached as far westwards as Fetter Lane, only just stopping short of the Temple Church, by Thursday the exhausted firefighters could pause to survey the damage. St Paul's was a ruin (fig. 18); eighty-seven churches had gone, along with the Guildhall, the Royal Exchange, the Custom House and fifty-two City Company halls. Thirteen thousand dwellings, housing London's population, had vanished. Of the great medieval city only a crescent of unburned buildings remained in the north-eastern corner. (fig. 22) Within it stood seven medieval churches – All Hallows-by-the-Tower, St Giles

Fig. 20 The remains of the effigy of Sir Thomas Heneage (d. 1594), Keeper of the Records in the Tower of London from 1577 and Queen Elizabeth's Vice-Chamberlain from 1589.

Fig. 21 The damaged effigy of Lady Elizabeth Wolley. Her husband, Sir John, was Latin Secretary to the Queen, and she served as a Lady of the Privy Chamber; the Queen probably was patron of the monument.

Cripplegate, St Olave Hart Street, St Helen Bishopsgate, St Andrew Undershaft, St Ethelburga and St Katherine Cree – and, most fortunately, Gresham College, which the City was able to use as its administrative headquarters.

The King immediately took control of the situation, issuing proclamations to reassure the citizens that London would be rebuilt and sending out into the countryside around to bring in supplies of bread and cheese to sustain everyone in the first desperate days. Within a week Wren had drawn up a plan for an ideal London: a perfect, geometrically ordered city which might be erected on the conveniently provided clean sheet that had been the capital (fig. 23). Four more such plans followed, from John Evelyn, from the mathematician Robert Hooke, from the City Surveyor, Peter Mills, and from a cartographer, Richard Newcourt.

None of these plans was accepted; the rebuilding of London was a strictly practical and realistic undertaking. In Wren's proposal the emphasis was placed on St Paul's. Leaving the Cathedral on its own site but realigning it slightly, he suggested opening up a triangular space to the west to maximise the dignity of the building on the elevation of Ludgate Hill. He continued the lines of the triangle eastwards, giving two main thoroughfares across the City. The northern street led to an enlarged Royal Exchange, with the Post Office, the Mint and banks and goldsmiths grouped around it – the Bank of England did not yet exist. Wren's plan linked God with Mammon, the spiritual balanced against the worldly. One thing shows clearly: to Wren, St Paul's was the most important building in London.

It was essential to get on with the rebuilding as other cities might have taken the commercial lead and replaced London as a centre of trade. A Commission for Rebuilding, with six Commissioners – three chosen by the King and three by the City – was appointed on 4 October 1666. The King appointed Wren, Hugh May and Roger Pratt; the City chose Hooke, Mills and Edward Jerman, the Master of the Carpenters' Company. Some wise decisions were made. London was to be rebuilt on its original plan but in stone, like Paris. Streets were to be paved and, wherever possible, widened. Obstructions, such as water conduits and market buildings, were to be moved out of roadways. Efforts were made to improve hygiene. London would cease to be a medieval city and would become a modern one.

Once begun, the work of clearing the ashes and ruins went on with amazing speed. Hooke, Mills and an experienced surveyor, John Oliver, were charged with the measuring of every plot of land. The Fire Court was set up to adjudicate disputes. Within three years the Royal Exchange was functioning once more; within seven, 8,000 houses had been rebuilt and London was operating again.

A special imposition, the Coal Tax, was levied on fuel entering the Port of London. A percentage of this revenue was set aside specifically for the rebuilding of St Paul's, but the tax was intended also to provide resources for the rebuilding of other churches and public buildings. Although money came in slowly, it was a reliable supply, and one that was collected at the point where it was needed.

Fig. 22 Wenceslaus Hollar's map of London and the suburbs after the Fire, 1666. The portion left white shows the extent of the damage; the positions of the churches are marked, though only ruins remain.

OVERLEAF:
Fig. 23 Wren's plan for a reformed London, presented to Charles II within a week of the Fire being brought under control, swept away the medieval tangle of streets and alleys, replacing them with broad geometrical thoroughfares.

As the Non-execution of this noble Plan must be regretted by all who see it, One cannot help wishing, That a proper Advantage was made of every Opportunity which Accident offers, or which arises from unavoidable Dilapidations & other concurrent Causes of Neglect & Desertion, to retrieve as much of it as can be retrievd; or, at least, to adopt the like Principles of Beauty, Elegancy, and Utility, which might be gradually effected perhaps, by means of a standing Commission, founded by Parliamentary Authority, & entrusted in proper Hands, for inspecting & condemning old useless Buildings, and regulating new ones. In all great & opulent City's Situation & Disposition are the first Things to be consider'd. The Situation of London cannot be mended; but as the Plan before us demonstrates, the Disposition of it may. Under ye head of Disposition all ye Requisits of Light, Air, Cleanliness, Safety, Ease of Communication, & every other Species of Commodiousness, as well as of Splendor and Magnificence are comprehended. A good Disposition costs no more than a bad one. The same may be said of Structures of all kinds. National Grandeur may be manifested & conducted without any Injury to private Property. And whoever reflects that Rome subsists at this Day on ye Remains of her ancient Majesty * (which still inflame the Curiosity and command the Admiration of Mankind) must al—

* Upwards of 50,000 is annually spent there by English Gentlemen

To the Consideration of ye Rt Honble ye Lord Mayor, ye Court this Plan, reduced from the Original of Sr Christopher Wren,

Map labels:
Clerkenwell
Charter House Square
Long Lane
Chick Lane
Smithfield
Hosier Lane
Cripple Gate
Holborn
Hatton Street
Holborn Bridge
Pye Corner
Aldersgate
Fetter Lane
Newgate
Lincolns Inn Fields
Lincolns Inn
Cursitors Alley
Chancery Lane
St Dunstans Church
St Pauls
Piazza
Piazza
Fleet Bridge
Ludgate
Temple Barr
Wood
London Wall
Wich Street
Markt
Strand
Temple Garden
Bridge
Key
Bridewell
Dock
Canal
The Grand Terras with the Public Halls.
Queen

That part of the Plan strongly shadow'd, shews ye extent of ye Conflagration, with St Christophers Design for Rebuilding the same, the Churches are mar'd thus ☩, and Markets thus ☿.

J. Gwynn Delin.

J. Wale.

EXPLANATION

From ye remaining part of Fleet-street which escaped the Fire, about St Dunstan's Church, a streight & wide Street crosses ye Valley, passing by the Northside of Ludgate Prison, & thence in a direct Line thro' ye whole City terminates at Tower Hill; but before it descends into ye Valley where ye Great Sewer runs, it opens into a Round Piazza, ye Center of Eight Ways, where at one station we see (I) streight forward quite thro' ye City; (II) Obliquely towards ye right hand, to ye beginning of ye

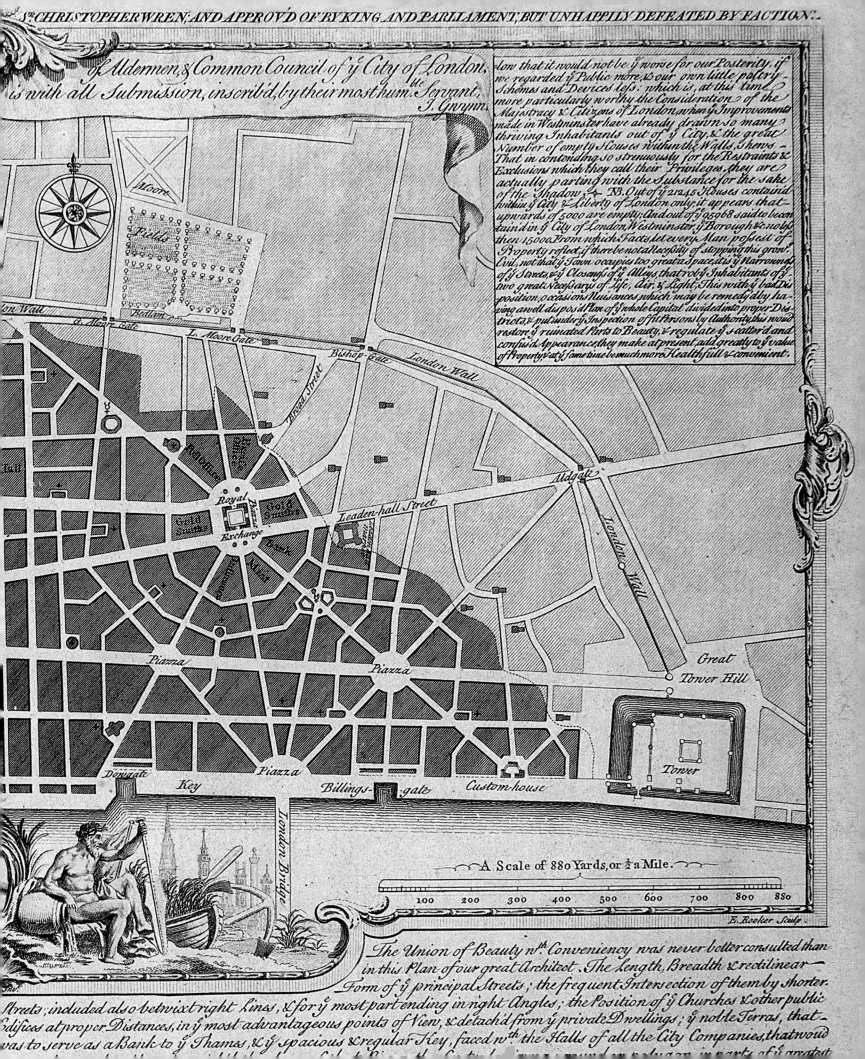

4

PLANNING
ST PAUL'S

REN'S preliminary planning of St Paul's Cathedral took nine years, from 1666 to 1675; the building of it extended over another thirty-six, till 1711. Mercifully, the architect had both the health and tenacity of purpose to carry the task through to the end in spite of all the difficulties – structural, financial and political – that from time to time hampered the realisation of his creation. It was the first cathedral to be completed in its architect's own lifetime.

His concept was as clearly fixed in his mind as it was amazing. The essential feature, the dome, was already present in the pre-Fire drawings made in the spring of 1666. The inspiration – the sheer excitement of it shows in every line – came from what Wren had seen in Paris, and the suggestion was very practical. The fall of the spire, just over a century earlier, had damaged and weakened the supports of the tower; the scaffolding inserted by Inigo Jones had been torn out and sold off on Parliament's orders, with the result that the vaulting of the south transept had collapsed. The 'noble cupola' of which Wren dreamed and Evelyn approved would be a lighter structure, one that the venerable medieval masonry might safely support but which would give London's cathedral an adornment of Renaissance distinction and European modernity. Something similar had happened, centuries before, at his uncle's cathedral of Ely: in 1322 the central tower had crashed down and been replaced by the octagon, much of which was built of timber and so far lighter.

Even in the confused aftermath of the Fire, Wren did not forget his dome. On the plan that he presented to Charles II within a week of the disaster there is an outline sketch of a new Cathedral. It appears to be a building in three parts: a circular, domed quire with a substantial square nave and a western portico reminiscent of Inigo Jones's work.

The six Commissioners for Rebuilding London were appointed on 4 October 1666. In the first months of the following year Wren provided a three-page report on the condition of the ruined Cathedral, with the suggestion that a temporary place of worship could be contrived towards the west end of the building so that services might continue while plans were being made for the restoration or rebuilding.

For the next eighteen months the authorities – ecclesiastical, political and civic – argued about whether the medieval fabric could be restored or whether it was damaged beyond repair. Wren stood aside from the debate; he had more than enough to do elsewhere in the City a well as the astronomy lectures that he continued to give at Oxford.

On 25 April 1668 Sancroft, the Dean, wrote to Wren at Oxford:

What you whispered in my ear at your last coming hither is now come to pass. Our work at the west end of St Paul's is fallen about our ears. Your quick eye discerned the walls and

BELOW:
Fig. 25 Wren's penknife with its sheath. In the days when pens were made from the quills of geese, such a knife was a necessary piece of equipment.

SIR CHR. WREN.
Late Surveyor General of
the Royal Buildings.
He died the 25th of Feby 1723, aged 91.

G. Kneller p.

pillars gone off from their perpendiculars and, I believe, other defects too which are now exposed to every common observer. About a week since, we being at work about the third pillar from the west end on the south side, which we had new cased with stone where it was most defective, almost up to the chapiter [sic], a great weight falling from the high wall so disabled the vaulting of the side aisle by it that it threatened a sudden ruin so visibly that the workmen presently removed and the next night the whole pillar fell and carried scaffolds and all to the very ground. The second pillar (which you know is bigger than the rest) stands now alone with an enormous weight on the top of it; which we cannot hope should stand long and yet we dare not venture to take it down.

He begged Wren to come 'with all possible speed' and concluded:

You will think fit, I know, to bring with you those excellent draughts and designs you formerly favoured us with; and in the meantime, till we enjoy you here, consider what to

Fig. 26 Wren's design for a cathedral planned like a Greek Cross, a basilica, with four equal arms and an imposing dome over the central space. There were to be porticoes on three sides.

Fig. 27 Drawn section through the Greek Cross model. Wren was still searching for the right way to construct the dome, and the design shows an inner and outer shell. The clergy found the basilica shape unsympathetic to the Anglican liturgy.

advise that may be for the satisfaction of his Majesty and the whole nation, an obligation so great and so public that it must be acknowledged by better hands that those of –
Your very affectionate friend and servant,
W. SANCROFT

Wren replied three days later, confidently and almost jocularly:

I received your account of the fate of Old Paul's and I must comfort you as I would a friend for the loss of his great Grandfather, by saying in the course of Nature you could not enjoy him, so many and so evident were to me the signs of its ruin when last I viewed the building.

He assured the Dean that he would be in London early the following week, 'bringing the old designs with me'.

The sight of further damage to the already desolate building was sobering. The magnitude

of the effort that would be involved in a complete rebuilding was bewildering. Ever practical and prudent, Wren realised that finance was the key to any future cathedral:

> I think it is silver upon which the foundation of any work must be first layed, lest it sink whilst it is yet rising. When you have found out the largeness and security of this sort of foundation, I shall presently resolve you what fabric it will bear.

Sancroft's reply was surprising. On 2 July 1668 he wrote again to Oxford, assuring Wren, 'without you [we] can do nothing'. He continued:

> I am therefore commanded to give you an invitation hither in his Grace's name and the rest of the Commissioners', with all speed, that we may prepare something to be proposed to his Majesty (the design of such a choir at least as may be a congruous part of a greater and more magnificent work to follow), and then for the procuring contributions to defray

this we are so sanguine as not to doubt of it, if we could but once resolve what we would do and what that would cost. So that the only part of your letter we demur to is the method you propound of declaring first what money we would bestow and then designing something just of that expense; for quite otherwise, the way their Lordships resolve upon is to frame a design handsome and noble, and suitable to all the ends of it and to the reputation of the City and the nation, and to take it for granted that money will be had to accomplish it.

Wren promptly put his Oxford affairs in order and set out for London. On 25 July a warrant was issued to demolish the tower and choir of Old St Paul's to make way for the new building, whatever shape it might take.

Recognition of his labours and his merits was not slow in coming. On 28 March 1669 Charles II appointed Wren Surveyor-General of the King's Works, at a salary of £200 a year. The Surveyor's first action was to secure an embargo on the export of stone from the Isle of

Fig. 30 South elevation of the Warrant Design. A portico at the west end is still there, on the left-hand side of the drawing, in memory of Inigo Jones's earlier achievement.

Portland; he realised that natural resources needed to be conserved and husbanded if a cathedral were ever to be built. What he cannot have known was how manifold the tasks would be that his royal master would lay on him in the years to come.

Made prosperous by his new salary, and with official quarters in Whitehall Palace, Wren was now in a position to marry. His bride was Faith Coghill, whom he had known for many years since her family lived at Bletchingdon, where he had spent his boyhood in his brother-in-law's rectory. Only one love letter survives. Faith had dropped her watch into salt water; her love had it repaired and returned it to her with a letter couched in a high-flown, poetical vein, but with a postscript more revealing of the scientist and the real man than the main text:

> *Madam. – The artificer having never before mett with a drowned watch, like an ignorant*
> *physician has been soe long about the cure that he hath made me very unquiet that your*
> *commands should be soe long deferred; however, I have sent the watch at last and envie*
> *the felicity of it, that it should be soe neer your side, and soe often enjoy your Eye, and be*
> *consulted by you how your time shall passe while you employ your hand in your excellent*
> *workes. But have a care of it, for I put such a Spell into it that every Beating of the Ballance*

Fig. 31 The Warrant Design was a compromise. It retained the lines of the medieval Cathedral with its long nave, and with the spire perched uncomfortably on top of Wren's dome.

will tell you 'tis the pulse of my Heart which labours as much to serve you and more trewly than the watch; for the watch I believe will sometimes lie, and sometimes perhaps be idle and unwilling to goe, having received so much injury by being drenched in that briny bath, that I dispair it should ever be a trew servant to you more. But as for me (unless you drown me too in my teares) you may be confident that I shall never cease to be,

Your most affectionate humble servant,
CHR. WREN

I have put the watch in a box that it might take noe harm, and wrapt it about with a little leather, and that it might not jog, I was fain to fill up the corners either with a few shavings or wast paper.

They were married on 7 December 1669 in the Temple Church and went to live in Wren's 'neatly furnished rooms' in Whitehall Palace.

A son, Gilbert, was born in October 1672; named, it may be guessed, after Gilbert Sheldon, he was christened at St Martin-in-the-Fields, but Robert Hooke's diary reveals that at a year old the child was seized with convulsions and that he died the following March.

A second son, Christopher, was born in February 1675; before the boy was a year old, he was motherless, for Faith was taken with smallpox late in August that year and died. Christopher grew up to be his father's companion and biographer.

Wren went on with his work. By the autumn of 1669, still mindful of financial constraints, he had produced what is now known as the First Design, developed from the little sketch on his post-Fire plan for a remodelled City. In March 1670 he presented a wooden model for consideration, parts of which survive and can be seen in the Trophy Room in St Paul's.

This design was felt to be 'not stately enough'; St Paul's was, after all, the metropolitan cathedral, and, some insisted, 'for the Honour of the Nation, and City of London, it ought not to be exceeded in Magnificence, by any Church in Europe'. So Wren set to work again, as his son described in *Parentalia*:

> *After this, in order to find what may satisfy the World, the Surveyor drew several Sketches meerly for Discourse-sake, and observing the Generality were for Grandeur, he endeavour'd to gratify the Taste of the Connoiseurs and Criticks, with something coloss [sic] and beautiful, with a Design antique & well studied, conformable to the best Stile of the Greek and Roman Architecture.*

This second design was the shape of a Greek cross, with equal arms, a central dome resting on eight piers, a small circular quire, and porticoes to the west, south and north (figs 26 and 27). Drawings were shown to Charles II by November 1672, and early the following year Wren told Hooke that a library and a more imposing portico were to be added to the west end. Wren and his draughtsman, Edward Woodroffe, started on another set of drawings, for what was to become known as the Great Model.

By this time Parliament had passed the Rebuilding Acts, and from 1670 money had begun to come in from the Coal Tax. In these early stages of the reconstruction both money and encouragement were readily available.

While these plans were being considered, the demolition of the medieval fabric was beginning. It was a daunting task. The medieval vaulting had risen to 93 feet (28 m) above the quire; the tower above the crossing had soared to 245 feet (73 m). When intact, the old Cathedral had been awe-inspiring; now, in its ruin, it was terrifying.

Perched on the walls, high in the air, or balancing on makeshift platforms hung between scaffolding poles, the labourers hacked away at the masonry with pickaxes. Pepys, walking by on 14 September 1668, felt seasick at the sight of falling stones. Three men were killed in these early stages of the work; the accounts show entries for inquests and shrouds and coffins, and money for the widows, to tide them over. Wren devised a battering-ram with a steel spike that was operated by thirty labourers; it worked, but slowly, and the men were exhausted.

Determined to hasten the demolition, Wren sent to the Tower of London for a gunner, expert in the laying of mines. A hole was dug into the foundations of the pillar at the north-west angle of the crossing, the charge was calculated and a train of gunpowder leading to it was lit. There was a muffled sound, the mass of stonework rose in the air and then collapsed on to its own foundations. People rushed out of their houses, thinking it was an earthquake, but no harm had been done to anyone.

The rest of the tower was demolished in a similar manner, but when it came to the pillars of the nave Wren was absent on official business, and his instructions were not followed precisely. Stones flew all over the Churchyard, one of them smashing a window and alarming the occupants. After that, there were no more explosions; the work had to proceed by hand, slowly.

By September 1673 Wren was preparing more drawings for the Great Model. By the next month William Cleere and his son Richard began the work of carving it on a scale of 1.24 inches (3.8 cm) to the foot (30.5 cm) (figs 28 and 29). Before it was finished, it had cost about £600, equivalent to the price of building a substantial merchant's house on a prime site such as Cheapside. Made of oak and plaster, originally painted stone colour inside and out, it stood 13 feet (3.95 m) high, measuring 13 feet 1 inch (3.97 m) from east to west and 20 feet 11 inches (6.36 m) across the transepts. It rested on raised trestle tables in what had once been the Chapter House, now patched up after the fire damage to provide shelter for this precious exemplar.

The model was large enough to be viewed from inside, so that the viewer might feel he was in the real building. Robert Hooke saw it complete – 'To Paules saw Module finished painting and guilding', he wrote in his diary – on 8 August 1674. An additional woodcarver, Stephen Cheele, had just been paid £3 12s. for eighteen little figures to stand around and in the structure; none of these survives.

It was to this design that Charles II gave his approval. On 12 November 1672 he had issued his Royal Commission for Rebuilding St Paul's, and two days later, at an early morning ceremony in Whitehall, he knighted Wren as a demonstration of his confidence in the architect. Wren went at once to Oxford to resign his professorship in astronomy. From now on, he was pledged to architecture alone.

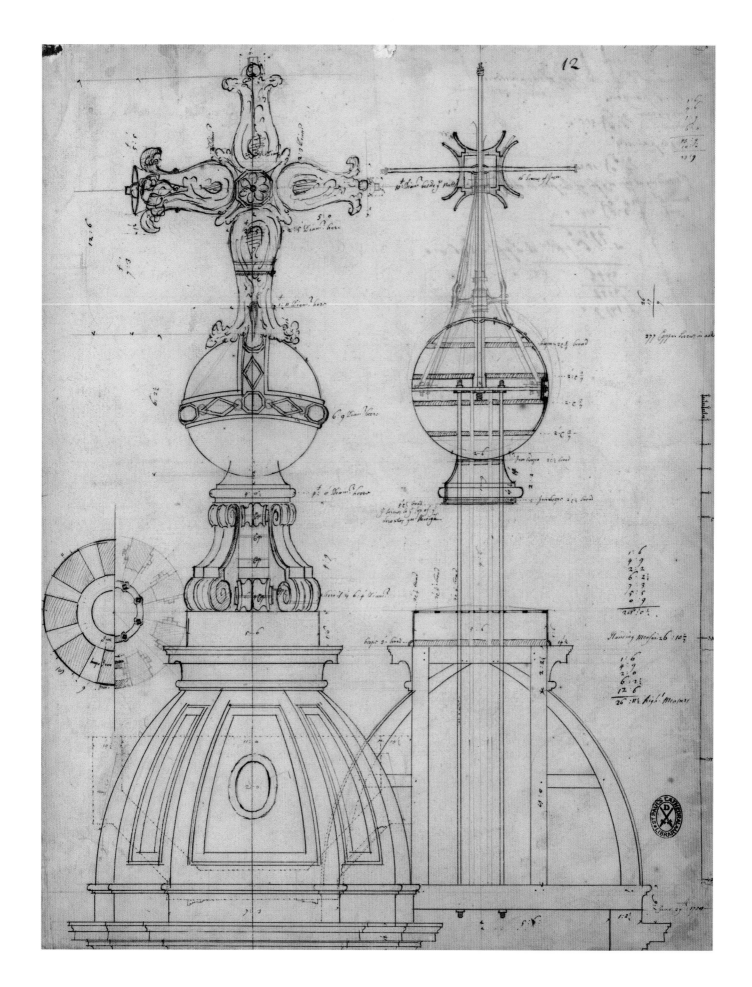

With its geometrical order and dignity, this design was the one dearest to the architect. But the clergy of St Paul's, once they could see clearly what was intended, began to have their doubts. St Paul's was the first Protestant cathedral to be built in England. It is essential to understand that memories of the Civil War, fought between 1642 and 1649, were still present in all men's minds. One of the prime causes of those wars was religion, and in particular the liturgy, the words and the ordering of the service, and the use or abandonment of the Book of Common Prayer. The shape of the Cathedral had to express the sequence and arrangement of the service. Blood had been shed; men had died for this. None of the clergy – neither Gilbert Sheldon (who by now was Archbishop of Canterbury), nor the King, Wren's patron, nor even the Dean, Wren's friend William Sancroft – could allow their regard for Wren to keep them silent when they realised that the Church of England service simply would not fit comfortably into such an untraditional design.

Wren was bitterly disappointed. His son Christopher, writing years later, recorded:

Thus much is specified, upon Recollecction, that the Surveyor in private Conversation, always seem'd to set a higher Value on his Design, than any he had made before or since; as what was labour'd with more Study and Success; and (had he not been over-rul'd by those, whom it was his Duty to obey), what he would have put in Execution with more Chearfulness, and Satisfaction to himself than the latter.

There was a further, technical objection to this cherished design. Its dome rested equally on eight great piers which would all have had to be built at once. An acceptance of the Great Model would commit the government to a financial outlay that could not readily be estimated. Moreover, no part of the building could be used till the whole was finished, at some unspecified time in the future. Something more practical was required, so that one part at least could be completed and used, thereby giving encouragement that the whole would be achieved one day. Expediency demanded another design.

With money starting to dribble in from the Coal Tax, it was essential to make some beginning. Wren and Woodroffe went back, yet again, to their drawing boards and produced another, more conventional, design, with a long nave and a spire on top of the dome instead of a lantern (figs 40 and 41). Charles gave his approval for this, the Warrant Design, on 14 May 1675. 'From that time', wrote the architect's son:

the Surveyor resolved to make no more Models, or publickly expose his Drawings, which (as he had found by Experience) did but lose Time, & subjected his Business many Times, to incompetent Judges. By these Means, at last, the Scheme of the present mighty Structure (different in some Manner from the former, & preferable in his Majesty's own Judgement, upon After-thoughts) was no sooner concluded on, and ordered by his Majesty, but begun and prosecuted by his Surveyor, with Vigour, in the Year 1675. And the King was pleas'd to allow him the Liberty in the Prosecution of his Work, to make some Variations, rather ornamental, than essential, as from Time to Time he should see proper; and to leave the Whole to his own Management.

In effect, Charles was determined to give his Surveyor freedom of action; the King had complete faith in Sir Christopher. Wren immediately began to rework his drawings. The Penultimate Design shortens the length of the nave by two bays, making it equal with the quire, and shows a lighter, more graceful dome. Before the masons' contracts were awarded for work to start in July 1675, Wren went over his plans yet again to produce the Definitive Design (fig. 32). Nine years of thought, negotiation and drawing had gone into the evolution of the design of St Paul's. Many details remained undecided, but the main scheme was settled.

Fig. 33 Details of lantern: cap, ball and cross, annotated by Wren's draughtsman, William Dickinson, and dated 1708.

5

BUILDING
ST PAUL'S

T HE TIME HAD COME to stake out the foundations for the quire and for the piers to
support the dome space at the eastern end of the newly cleared site. Sir Christopher,
needing to mark a particular spot, asked a labourer to fetch a stone. The man came
back with a fragment of a broken tombstone on which was carved one word, *RESURGAM* –
'I shall rise again.' The architect never forgot that omen; his son tells the story in *Parentalia*,
and it was clearly an incident from which Sir Christopher drew comfort when the obstacles
that arose during the long years of the rebuilding seemed insuperable.

Water, provided by the New River Company at £5 a year, had been laid on at the site
since March 1668. Thousands of loads of rubbish and rubble had been cleared away by teams
of labourers. Night watchmen were essential from the start, their guardianship enforced by
'2 great mastiffe Doggs', for whom meat was regularly provided; tools and building materials
were valuable, and pilfering was a problem. An Acquittance Book records expenditure from
immediately after the Fire till September 1675; from 1 October strict building accounts were
kept, inspected monthly by Wren and audited annually. From these the building of the new
Cathedral can be followed, the first masons' contracts being awarded in the summer of 1675.

The foundation stone was laid on 21 June 1675. Unlike the ceremony and fanfares that
had accompanied inaugurations at the Royal Exchange, when each main pillar had been laid
by a member of the royal family, no dignitaries attended St Paul's. The first stone was set in
place by Thomas Strong, the Master Mason, and by John Longland, the Master Carpenter.
Characteristically, Wren gave the honours to his workmen.

By this time some twenty-five City churches had been completed or were under way,
and Wren had a good idea of whom he should employ on the great undertaking. Each master mason or carpenter would retain perhaps twenty or more skilled journeymen; he needed
to be able to manage a team and to be substantial enough financially to carry the business
side of the undertaking. Until the Fire, guild regulations had been strict – a man had to be
free of the City of London (i.e. having served a seven-year apprenticeship there and been
admitted to the appropriate Company after paying his dues); now, in the emergency of the
rebuilding, provincial craftsmen were made welcome in the capital – all that mattered was
their degree of skill.

The first contracts were awarded to Joshua Marshall and Thomas Strong. Marshall was
allotted both the north and south walls of the quire and the two huge stone bastions at its
west end, intended one day to support the dome. Strong was awarded the east wall with the
semicircular apse. Soon the pair were employing some sixty skilled journeymen, with a hundred labourers preparing the foundations and providing general support. A score of

Fig. 34 View down the nave,
looking towards the high altar.
In Wren's day, there would
have been no seating to
interrupt the pattern of the
flooring, probably designed by
William Dickinson.

carpenters set up scaffolding and centring for the arches. Capstans were made 'for winding up of great stones to the Masons'.

The office in the old Convocation House, now adapted to its new use, was made as welcoming as the limits of strict economy permitted: William Parris, the upholsterer, provided 62 yards (57 m) of 'green printed stuff at 2s a yard', and chairs were made ready, well padded with horsehair; there was a desk and bookcases, and shutters were set up at the windows. If the King were to drop in – as indeed he did from time to time – he would find a room far from luxurious but fit to receive him.

In all this activity the key person was Sir Christopher. Throughout it all he remained calm, cheerful, friendly but impartial, and confident in the work, his workmen and himself. At this stage Charles II was behind him, Gilbert Sheldon was Archbishop of Canterbury, Henry Compton, who had been Wren's companion in Paris a decade earlier and who had fought for Charles I in the Civil War, was Bishop of London, and William Sancroft was Dean. The money from the Coal Tax had been allowed to accumulate during the years of planning, and to it had been added substantial bequests from those who had not lived to see the work done – Archbishops Laud and Juxon, and Dr Henchman, the previous Bishop of London. But once the spending of these resources had started, they would soon be depleted, so with the King's authority a special appeal was made in 1677 to the City and to the whole country, which brought good results.

While the appeal was in progress, Archbishop Sheldon died, and the King appointed a very reluctant Sancroft to the primacy. An austere, devout man, Sancroft preferred the comparative anonymity of his deanery to the dignity of Lambeth Palace, with the magnificent new hall that Archbishop Juxon had built. But from Wren's point of view good came of it, for while Sancroft remained his friend, to the Deanery came another supporter, Edward Stillingfleet. John Tillotson, Dean of Canterbury, Fellow of the Royal Society and Wren's friend, became a new residentiary, or residential canon. At the same time William Holder, Wren's brother-in-law, joined the clergy of the Cathedral, so now the architect's favourite sister, Susanna, was nearby, ready to give support as the building work slowly progressed.

At this stage the main problem lay in obtaining the right stone in large enough blocks. The most appropriate material came form the Isle of Portland, an area of solid rock linked to the mainland of the Dorset coast by a narrow isthmus. Inigo Jones had used this stone – smooth, white, soft enough to carve but weathering well after exposure to the elements – in his recasing

Fig. 35 Determined to avoid further criticism and interference, Wren built the Cathedral behind screens of wattle. This engraving by Sutton Nicholls was issued in an attempt to assuage curiosity.

of St Paul's. Although the island was Crown property, the inhabitants had the right to dig stone for themselves but not to sell it. The islanders – for such they considered themselves to be – were a race apart and a law unto themselves; whatever the physical difficulties might be in obtaining stone, the problems of dealing with the people were significant too.

When a substantial block had been dug, it had to be loaded on to a cart or trolley and dragged to the pier, which Inigo Jones had had built at the enormous cost of £700, on the south side of the island. There it had to be loaded by crane on to a light vessel and from that transferred to a larger ship moored further out; great care was needed, for immersion in sea water would stain the stone. Once on board, the cargo could be sailed round the coast, up the Thames and unloaded at St Paul's quay, whence it had to be dragged or winched up the steep incline of St Peter's Hill to the Cathedral precinct. For a really large stone, this last stage could take more than a week, with the resulting disruption to the movement of people and goods. The rebuilding of St Paul's was something that affected all the citizens of London.

With matters running smoothly in the City, Wren married for the second time. His bride was Jane FitzWilliam; her father was Baron FitzWilliam, of Lifford in Ireland, though the family came from Northamptonshire. The wedding took place on 24 February 1677 at the Chapel Royal in Whitehall Palace, and a daughter was born to them in November. She was called Jane, like her mother, and grew up to be Sir Christopher's favourite child. A second child, William, followed in June 1679; he had learning difficulties, and the proper care of 'poor Billy' was a matter of family concern throughout the sixty years of his life. Lady Wren died on 4 October 1680. Not one letter has survived of any that may have passed between her and Sir Christopher, but Robert Hooke mentions her several times in his laconic diary, noting once that he supped on bacon and beans at Wren's house and recording also that she asked him for 'Mahomet's book'. This must have been a collection of letters, translated into Latin, by the eleventh Sultan of the Turks, so perhaps Lady Wren was an intellectual

companion for her husband. She was buried in St Martin-in-the-Fields, beside the first Lady Wren. Sir Christopher did not marry again.

But just when things seemed to be going well at St Paul's, misfortunes began. In April 1678 Joshua Marshall died in the prime of life, leaving his business to his young, inexperienced and headstrong widow, who soon managed to fall out with Wren – something of a feat in itself. Marshall had been carrying a major share of the work, and three master masons were needed to shoulder his responsibilities: Edward Pierce, Jasper Latham and Thomas Wise. No sooner was that settled than Thomas Strong died, but he was able to leave the business to his much younger brother Edward, in whose care all went well.

In the outside world of politics there were troubles too, which eventually would impinge on St Paul's enclave. Matters centred on religion. Charles and his sweet and dignified Portuguese wife, Catherine of Braganza, were childless, so the heir to the throne was the King's younger brother James, the Duke of York, who was a Roman Catholic. There were rumours of plots to murder the King, and Parliament brought in a bill to exclude the Duke from succession to the throne. The Bishop of London, always a military man at heart – he had played a soldier's part in the Civil War – voted for the Bill, thereby bringing St Paul's into royal disfavour.

Charles dissolved Parliament, which meant that the Coal Tax, due to end in 1687, could not be extended or increased to help the Cathedral, where once again funds were running low. Even John Evelyn, Wren's lifelong friend and supporter, began to doubt whether it would ever be finished. The situation worsened when the King, at loggerheads with London, confiscated the City Charter; the Aldermen and Common Council thought about London's position rather than St Paul's predicament.

Work slowed down; in winter the masonry had to be boarded over. Nevertheless, Wren pressed on doggedly, and his devoted team continued to give support. Then, suddenly and quite unexpectedly, in February 1685 Charles II was taken ill, and within less than a week he was dead, at the age of fifty-four. James II ascended the throne. Parliament was summoned, with Sir Christopher now elected as the Member for Plympton St Maurice in Devon – he was determined that there should be someone in the assembly to speak up for St Paul's. The Coal Tax was extended to 1700, and the proportion due to the Cathedral was increased threefold, from about £6,000 a year to something in the region of £18,500.

Work began again in earnest, and contracts were prepared for the west end. Latham and Pierce, who had proved temperamental and difficult, were not offered work, which went instead to the younger Thomas Wise and his partner Thomas Hill, to Edward Strong and to two new men, John Thompson and Samuel Fulkes, who proved faithful members of Wren's team. The City, realising that something really was happening behind the scaffolding, began to take an interest again (fig. 35).

And then, as before, the political situation worsened. The unpopularity of James II increased, and an invitation was sent to his son-in-law William of Orange to come to England to try to readjust matters. William landed with an army at Torbay in November 1688; James summoned his regiments and advanced to Reading, where most of his men deserted him. The King fled from London, only to be captured, and then, with William's tacit connivance, he was allowed to escape and take refuge in France. Parliament declared that he had abandoned the throne and offered the Crown jointly to William and his wife, Mary, James's elder daughter.

People wondered how the new regime would regard Sir Christopher; he and his work were so closely identified with the previous Stuart monarchs. But Mary was a Stuart too, and perhaps she found comfort in the company of the serene, reassuring architect, for she was haunted with guilt for having driven her father from his throne. Every autumn she sent a buck from Windsor Forest; Wren and his colleagues ate the venison and drank the Queen's health at the annual 'passing of the books' each Michaelmas.

Fig. 38 The west front in autumn framed by the branches of a plane tree.

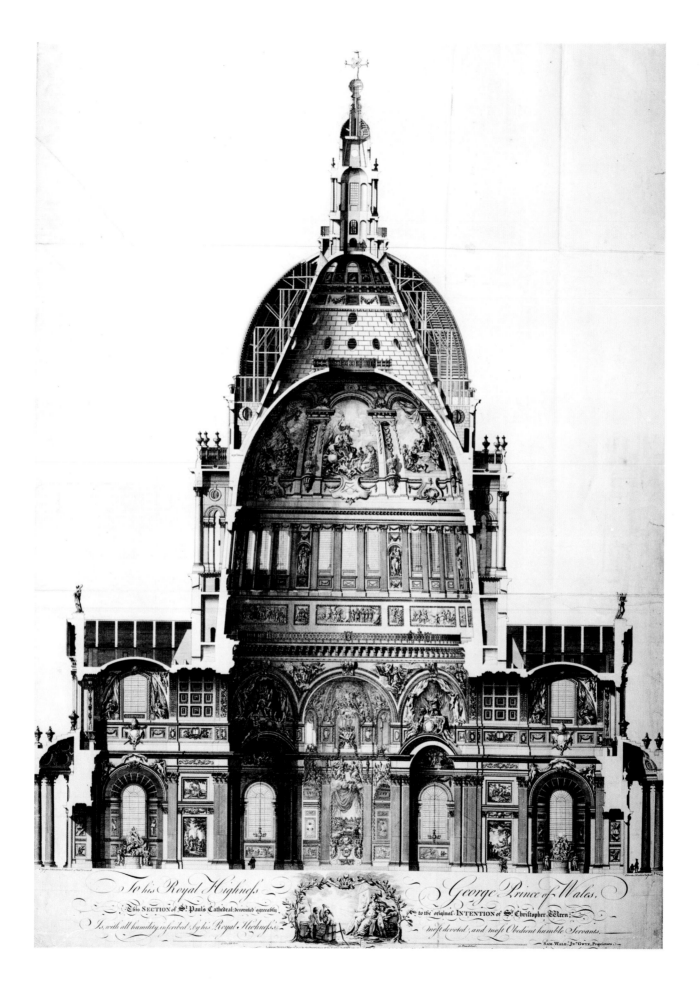

To his Royal Highness George Prince of Wales.

This SECTION of St Paul's Cathedral, decorated agreeable to the original INTENTION of St Christopher Wren; Is, with all humility inscribed, by his Royal Highness's most devoted, and most Obedient humble Servants.

SAM. WALE; JNO GWYN, Proprietors.

OPPOSITE:
Fig. 39 St Paul's Cathedral, a section through the building engraved by Samuel Wale and John Gwyn, 1755. This shows the position of Sir James Thornhill's paintings on the inner dome and illustrates the construction of the brick cone supporting the outer dome.

RIGHT:
Fig. 40 Above the dome, the Golden Gallery encircles the lantern, which is topped with a ball and cross; the weather-beaten originals were faithfully replaced by C. R. Cockerell, Surveyor to the Fabric of St Paul's. The cross is 365 ft (111 m) from the ground.

OVERLEAF:
Fig. 41 Looking through the inner oculus of the dome to the lunettes that let light into the cone. Sir James Thornhill's false coffering is spectacularly successful.

Even so, the world was changing. The reign of Charles II had been an attempt to patch together the fabric of a society shattered by civil war. Now it was torn apart again by William's assumption of the throne. A new generation was growing up; there were people who regarded Sir Christopher as an old man, and who were jealous of him.

One of them was an amateur architect, William Talman, who fancied his own talents and who coveted the Surveyorship. When a new building designed by Wren at Hampton Court collapsed, killing some workmen, he reported it as gross negligence on the part of the architect; the report was signed by Pierce and Latham, angry that their contracts at St Paul's had not been renewed. Wren was cleared of all blame, but it was a sign that life might not be easy in the future.

Sir Christopher must have felt himself very alone now. His sister Susanna had died in the summer of 1688; he and William Holder had laid her to rest in the half-finished crypt of St Paul's. Sancroft refused to crown William king, was deprived of his archbishopric and retired to his family home in Fressingfield to pass his remaining years in quietude. Dean Tillotson

was, regretfully, promoted to the see of Canterbury. Only Henry Compton, Bishop of London, remained in position, ever supportive, and there was the building team, many of whom had grown up with the Cathedral.

Once again money ran short, and there were constant problems over supplies from Portland, for England, with William, Stadtholder of Holland as its King, was now at war with France, and the ships bearing stone needed an escort of men-of-war. However, the new king issued a fresh commission for the building to continue, and by the spring of 1693 work began on the roofing of the quire. The task was completed by the end of the year, and the fitting out of the interior was begun.

Before the end of 1694 two of Wren's staunchest supporters were dead: Archbishop Tillotson collapsed with a stroke on 18 November and died a few days later, while Queen Mary was stricken with smallpox the following month and died on 28 December. The nation mourned her with extraordinary but well-merited fervour.

More troubles followed. An enormous landslide on the Isle of Portland affected all transport of stone, and it took two visits by Wren's best masons and a third by Wren himself in May 1697 to get anything there moving again. Mercifully, the eight great stone arches to support the dome were already completed before the disaster occurred. The House of Commons, growing tetchy, suspended half of Wren's salary, reducing it to £100 till the work was completed. Westminster Abbey promptly appointed him to the Surveyorship of that building at a rate of £200, so he was not out of pocket. Sir Christopher allowed himself no complaints, but he made one small gesture, billing the building accounts for the pens, paper, ink and sand with which he had supplied the office for twenty years; the total came to £200.

In the autumn of 1697, when the building of the organ, by the German organ-builder 'Father' Bernard Smith, was well under way, Grinling Gibbons's woodwork in the quire was almost complete and Jean Tijou's wrought-iron screens were in place, the Cathedral received a private visit from Princess Anne, the daughter of James II and now heir to the throne. A deeply shy woman, she said little, but approved wholeheartedly of what she saw. The war with France had dragged to an end, both sides being exhausted, and it was decided that the

Fig. 43 Interior view across the west end by Robert Trevitt, showing mastery of perspective. Patronised by Wren, Trevitt was responsible for at least six views of the Cathedral.

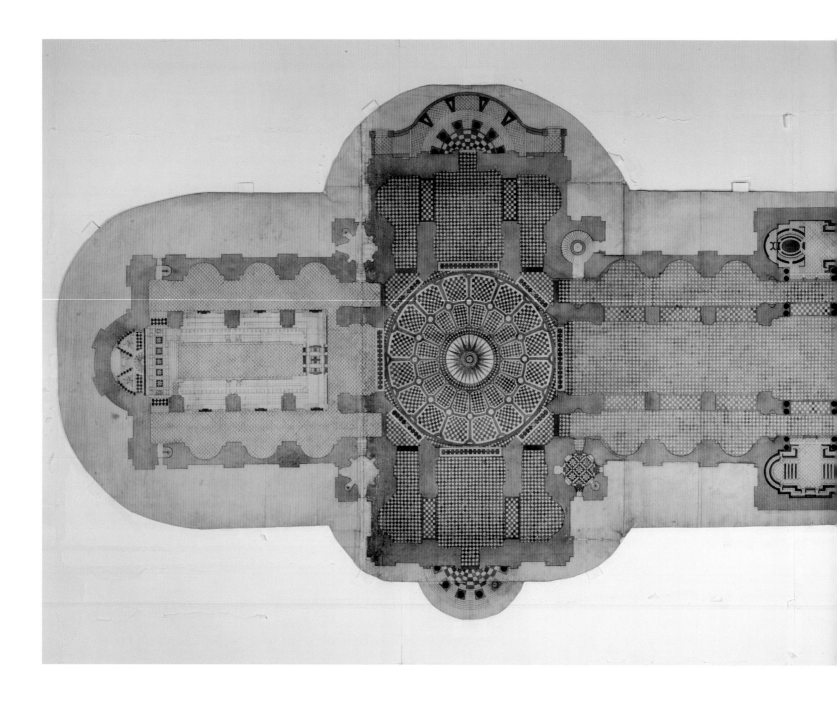

Fig. 44 Plan for the paving of
the nave, probably drawn by
William Dickinson after the
work was completed. The work
was carried out by William
Kempster.

completed quire should be used for the first time on 2 December for a thanksgiving service
for the Peace of Ryswick.

At the last minute King William decided not to attend, but no one seemed very
disappointed. The Lord Mayor was resplendent, and the Bishop of London preached a
triumphant sermon on the text 'I was glad when they said unto me: Let us go into the house
of the Lord'. The first morning service was held three days later, on Sunday, 5 December
1697. John Evelyn attended it with rejoicing; he tried to go back in the afternoon for another
look but found the crowds thronging the new building so dense that he could not get in a
second time. Now it was time to think about completing the west end and – at last – raising
the dome.

Before that could happen, on 8 March 1702 William III died from a fall from his horse
and a subsequent chill to his always delicate lungs. Anne became queen, one of the saddest
figures ever to fill the throne of England, for she had borne and lost numerous children. She

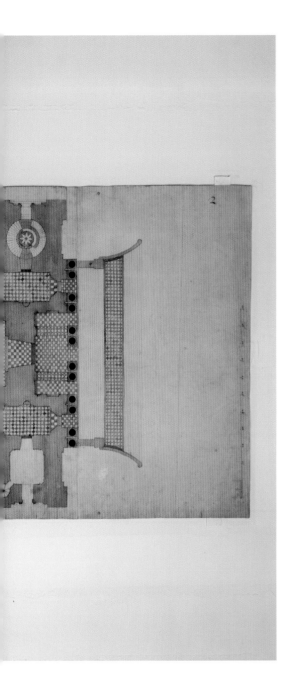

cherished St Paul's, returning to it again and again for thanksgiving services for the victories of John Churchill, later Duke of Marlborough, in the renewed war with France. In the year of William's death Wren suffered a further bereavement. His daughter Jane, his support and companion, died at the age of twenty-six and was buried in the crypt. Wren wrote her Latin epitaph, describing her as 'like her father, fond of learning, dutiful, kind, home-loving, an expert musician'. His favourite sculptor, Francis Bird, carved her memorial, showing her as St Cecilia, the patron saint of music, seated at the organ (fig. 36). Now there was only his work; the Cathedral had to be finished.

The problems remained the same – money and Portland stone. By the time the quire was complete, St Paul's was heavily in debt, but the principal contractors offered to work on unpaid, the debts to be treated as loans to the Cathedral until such time as they could be settled. The Coal Duty Act of 1702 renewed government support, and the work progressed slowly but steadily.

Portland was another matter. The landslide damage was repaired, but stone still arrived fitfully, water-damaged or cut to the wrong size, and there were repeated attempts to falsify the duty due, to the advantage of the islanders. Wren wrote to them:

> Though 'tis in your power to be as ungrateful as you will, yet you must not think that your insolence will be always borne with, and though you will not be sensible to the advantage you receive by the present working of the quarries yet, if they were taken from you, I believe you might find the want of them in very little time; and you may be sure that care will be taken both to maintain the Queen's right and that such only will be employed in the quarries as will work regularly and quietly, and submit to proper and reasonable directions, which I leave you to consider of.

Matters went more smoothly for a short while, but in a year or two trouble started again and continued to the end.

It remained to complete the west front and to raise the dome (fig. 38). Wren had wished to preserve or to reproduce Inigo Jones's noble portico, but that proved impossible. Then he hoped to install a single-storey entrance to the Cathedral, as he had shown it in the Great Model, with giant-sized pillars; but stones mighty enough for such an approach could not be obtained. At last he settled for a two-storey portico, with twelve great coupled columns for the base and eight above, supporting a pediment adorned with a relief, carved by Francis Bird, of the Conversion of St Paul. On either side rose the twin west towers, the southern one containing a clock designed and made by Langley Bradley, the northern one housing the four-ton bell Edward of Westminster, which since the days of Edward III had hung in the New Palace Yard just outside Westminster Hall.

Before the end of William's reign, work had begun on the dome. Wren divided the task into four equal sections, allotting them to Nathaniel Rawlins, Christopher Kempster and Ephraim Beauchamp, the younger Wise and Thomas Hill, and Edward Strong. The lofty spire, proposed a quarter of a century earlier as a finishing touch on the Warrant Design, was quietly forgotten.

Wren had had a problem with the dome, about which he had worried over the years. For it to be the dominating feature on the London skyline it had to rise steeply, massively above the building, but such a pitch would be jarring and discordant when viewed from within. Two domes were needed: the outer one lofty, the inner one shallower, tranquil, harmonious. Between them, hidden from all save those willing to undertake the ascent, was an inner dome, a cone made of brick, strong enough to support a lantern which, Wren had decided, must be substituted for the grotesque spire. It had to be firm enough to anchor the outer dome, which could now be made of timber covered with lead. The Duke of Newcastle donated ten massive oaks (fig. 39).

Wren judged it was time to let London know what he was doing. With the Commissioners' approval, he engaged Jan Kip, who came from Holland but who had been resident in London since William's arrival, and he engraved 200 copies of the ground-plan and northern prospect, while Simon Gribelin, from France, attended to the west front. The disappearance of the spire went unnoticed. The public rushed to buy these views as well as those undertaken later by Robert Trevitt, who depicted both the exterior and the interior (figs 42 and 43).

Work on the brickwork of the inner dome began in April 1705. Here Wren's engineering genius showed itself again for, as his son tells us, he devised a framework that was both scaffolding and centring. The new Master Carpenter, Richard Jennings, built it so skilfully and supervised the work so attentively that Wren awarded him an extra 50 guineas for his pains.

Under the Master Bricklayer Richard Billinghurst three dozen men worked patiently at the brick cone. The whole extraordinary structure had already been reinforced at its base with an iron chain about it, wrought by Thomas Coalburne and Thomas Robinson; now a second, even stronger, one was made by Jean Tijou and was added to bind the main structure, the cone and the inner dome together. Under Richard Jennings the carpenters toiled at the ribs of the outer dome while Edward Strong and his team laboured at the stone lantern.

Wren's intention was to cover the dome with sheets of lead. However, businessmen whose interests lay in the copper industry lobbied Parliament, and a Bill was brought in that copper should be the material employed. The material glows like gold when fresh but soon streaks and turns first black and then bright green, often unevenly. The effect would have been garish, at odds with the serenity of the stonework. Mercifully, when Parliament was dissolved, the subject was dropped. Work on the lead skin began almost immediately, with the Master Plumber Joseph Roberts in charge. The metal was laid in thick sheets: 'best Derbyshire lead', 12 pounds (5.4 kg) to the square foot (930 sq. cm).

By this time the delivery of materials to the upper reaches had become a serious problem. The stone, the timber, the lead – all had to be hauled up to where they were needed, and the charge for haulage had risen to 4s. 6d. a ton. Each Saturday Sir Christopher's slight frame was part of the burden. He was now in his seventies and to clamber up the stairs and scaffolding was beginning to be too severe an effort, so he too was hauled up in a basket.

At last, in the autumn of 1708, it was time to set the last stone on the lantern (fig. 40). The date is given variously, but may well have been 20 October, Sir Christopher's seventy-sixth birthday. His son Christopher, born the year in which the Cathedral had been begun, performed the topping-out ceremony, assisted by old Edward Strong, Master Mason, whose brother Thomas had laid the foundation stone. There was no grand ceremony, no royal personages, though lonely Queen Anne would certainly have rejoiced in her Surveyor's achievement. Neither politicians nor City dignitaries are recorded as attending – only the men who had toiled for so long. That was Sir Christopher's way, and those who worked for him respected and loved him for it.

Of those present, besides Wren, only Strong, Laurence Spencer, the Clerk of Works, and Henry Compton, Bishop of London, who on spring mornings in 1665 had ridden out with the future architect into the French countryside, could remember the commencement of the great task. All the rest – King Charles, Archbishops Sheldon and Sancroft, Wren's friend John Evelyn, his draughtsman Woodroffe, his masons Joshua Marshall and Thomas Strong, and Henry and William Cleere, who had carved the Great Model – were dead. To Wren had been granted length of life and strength of purpose to complete the task.

The next two years were spent in repairing cracks that had appeared and in finishing the interior; the laying of the marble floor was the major task (fig. 44). But then friction began

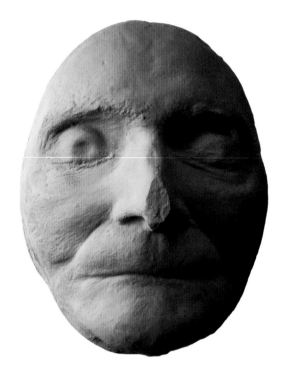

Fig. 45 Wren's death mask. He died on 25 February 1723, aged ninety-one. He had spent the day visiting his beloved Cathedral.

with the Cathedral clergy. There was a new, younger generation in the Chapter House, men to whom Inigo Jones had shrunk to an almost forgotten figure, to whom the Civil War with its principles and its violence had faded into tales told by a grandfather. Wren was an old man; his style of architecture, if magnificent, was old-fashioned. They considered that his share of the work was done, and that it was their responsibility to adorn and decorate the Cathedral in a modern manner. Wren planned to line the inner dome with mosaic or – if that were too costly – to have it painted with coffering in a profound perspective. The new Dean and Chapter had other ideas.

Sir Christopher's plans for a fresh, uncluttered laying out of the Churchyard were also thwarted (a problem with which planners still strive today). He suggested that the Churchyard should at least be surrounded by a wrought-iron fence, to be created by the Master Smith Thomas Robinson; the Cathedral clergy insisted on one of cast iron, provided by the possibly dishonest and certainly very expensive founder Richard Jones. Wren did succeed in appointing Francis Bird to carve a statue of Queen Anne to stand in front of the Cathedral, but the storm clouds gathered.

A pamphlet war broke out of dishonesty against Richard Jennings, the Master Carpenter for the dome, and suggestions that Sir Christopher had been insufficiently vigilant of late years. The Queen, ever Wren's loyal supporter, dissolved the Commission for the Rebuilding of the Cathedral and appointed a new one, from which all the Chapter clergy save the Dean were excluded; the Surveyor, properly in control once again, had the Churchyard put in order. A wrought-iron fence, worked by Jean Tijou himself, surrounded Queen Anne's statue. Wren applied for, and received, the arrears of salary that had been withheld. On 7 July 1713 both Houses of Parliament attended a thanksgiving service since the wars with France had ended, for the time being, with the Peace of Utrecht; the Queen was too ill to attend and died the following year. It was proper that her statue should stand before St Paul's, for she had defended it.

Once again there was a change of dynasty. The Hanoverians ascended the throne, and there was no one to stand up for the Cathedral or the ageing Surveyor. But Wren still held his official post and was still on the Commission; his consent still had to be obtained for any major changes or additions. The Chapter wanted a parapet around the summit of the body of the Cathedral. Wren replied that he had not designed one but did not argue, simply saying pointedly that 'Ladies think nothing well without an edging'. With Wren's approval Bird carved the statues to stand along the west front, St Paul on the apex of the pediment with St Peter and St James to the sides, and the four Evangelists to flank the western towers in pairs.

In 1718 scheming at Court deprived Wren of his life appointment as Surveyor-General at the Office of Works. He took it calmly and philosophically, and passed his remaining years in contentment in a small house that Queen Anne had granted him on Hampton Green, close to the royal palace. Every so often he came up to London to visit St Paul's and to sit under the dome. On one such visit, on 25 February 1723, he stayed in a house in St James's and there, at the age of ninety-one, he died quite peacefully, sitting in a chair by the fire after supper (fig. 45).

His sons, Christopher and 'poor Billy', buried him at the south-east end of St Paul's crypt, near to his daughter, sister and brother-in-law (fig. 46). A plain stone slab with a simple inscription covers the grave but on the wall his elder son set a tablet with its proud epitaph:

Lector, si monumentum requiris,Circumspice
'Reader, if you seek a monument, look about you.'

St Paul's itself is Wren's best memorial.

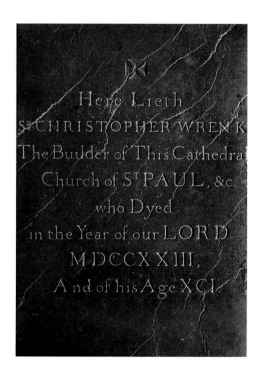

Fig. 46 The original inscription on Wren's grave. His son added another, more elaborate, with the familiar epitaph.

OVERLEAF:
Fig. 47 *The Thames on Lord Mayor's Day. Looking towards the City*, by Antonio Canaletto, c. 1747. The City's skyline is punctuated by the spires of Wren's churches, dominating it as they were to do for two and a half centuries.

6

DRAUGHTSMEN AND CRAFTSMEN

SIR CHRISTOPHER WREN was the architect of St Paul's, but he did not build the Cathedral single-handed. He needed a team of draughtsmen and a clerk of works, masons, sculptors, bricklayers, carpenters, joiners, woodcarvers, smiths, glaziers and – indispensably – labourers. Many of these are shadowy figures, though some of them, having served an apprenticeship on the Cathedral, moved on to other great achievements. A careful reading of the long series of detailed accounts, covering the entire history of the building, tells us something about several of the others.

The first name among those providing immediate support to Wren is that of Edward Woodroffe. In 1662 Woodroffe was appointed Surveyor to Westminster Abbey, a post he held till his death in 1675, and he joined Wren as a mature and experienced man with great skill in drawing; he may have worked with John Webb, Inigo Jones's assistant, nephew-in-law and, later, colleague. With Wren and Hooke, Woodroffe was one of the surveyors appointed to rebuild the City churches. Wren probably considered Woodroffe as his equal in all practical matters – he certainly had more experience than the architect. John Tillison, the Clerk of Works, writing to Dean Sancroft at his country house in Suffolk, told him:

> Dr Wren & Mr Woodroof [sic] have been the week last past in ye Convocation house, drawing the Lines of ye Designe of the church upon ye Table there, for ye Joyner's Directions for making ye new Modell.

The two men were clearly working together closely on Wren's most cherished proposal, and many of the most exquisite surviving drawings are in Woodroffe's hand. It was Woodroffe who designed the houses in Amen Court for the three Residentiary Canons of the Cathedral. In the late summer of 1675 he was taken ill, seemed to recover, relapsed and then died on 16 November, aged only fifty-four. He was buried in the cloisters of Westminster Abbey. With his death Wren and St Paul's had lost a good friend and supporter.

Woodroffe was replaced by John Oliver, a man of a most retiring disposition who, at the age of sixty, had a lifetime's experience behind him. He was a glazier by trade but, being exceptionally versatile, had trained himself to be a surveyor and as such, on Edward Jerman's death, became one of those appointed by the Corporation to supervise the rebuilding of the City. Oliver was involved in the building of the Monument, set up to commemorate the Great Fire, and at least one of the churches: St Mary Aldermary. When Jerman died in 1668, Oliver took over the rebuilding of the Mercers' Company Hall. He had considerable diplomatic skills, for it was he whom Wren sent to Portland in 1679 to negotiate with the obstreperous islanders. About 1680 he published a map of the rebuilt City. He retained his original skill for, at the age

Fig. 48 The sweep of the Dean's Staircase spirals upwards to the Library in two complete revolutions. The ironwork of the balustrade is by Jean Tijou.

Fig. 49 The choir stalls looking towards the east window, here framed by the baldacchino of the high altar.

of eighty-four, he presented a window that he had painted to Christ Church, Oxford. Oliver was Wren's trusty and trusted colleague, and when he died in November 1701 he was buried in the crypt of the Cathedral he had served faithfully for a quarter of a century. He was succeeded by Thomas Bateman, brisk and efficient but less diplomatic; the presentation of the accounts became immediately tighter and less informative.

Wren's office staff included John Tillison as Clerk of Works and Paymaster; Laurence Spencer was his assistant. Tillison went each week by coach to the Guildhall, where the money from the Coal Tax was deposited, to collect sufficient to pay the men's wages. It was also his duty to enter up the contract book. He took the roll-call for the workmen at 6 a.m., at noon and at 6 p.m. For this he received £20 a year over and above his wages of 12s. a week. He checked the arrival, the quantities and the sizes of stone, and all other building materials besides; on one occasion he too took part in an expedition to Portland. Quietly spoken and self-effacing, he was nevertheless always there when he was needed. When Tillison died in December 1685, Spencer took over the duties of Paymaster as well. He was one of the very few, besides Wren himself, who saw the first stone laid and attended the final topping-out ceremony.

Late in 1679, or early the following year, Nicholas Hawksmoor was appointed as a clerk. He was a competent and literate eighteen-year-old. Wren must have noticed that there was something unusual in the young man and began to employ him on making drawings. Hawksmoor gradually became an exceptional draughtsman; in March 1691 he was for the first time paid as such, at 1s. 8d. a day. In the summer of 1697 he accompanied Wren to Portland. By this time he had been made Clerk of Works for the new palace being built at Kensington and had undertaken, under Wren's watchful eye, a first commission, a Writing School for Christ's Hospital in the City.

Hawksmoor was an extraordinary architect: powerful, imaginative and dramatic. In 1711 an Act was passed to build fifty new churches in the outer suburbs of the City and Westminster; in fact, only twelve of them were ever realised, but of that dozen Hawksmoor was responsible for six. These structures reflect his temperament, which was deeply gloomy and depressive; his work was forbidding, awe-inspiring and, sometimes, frightening. He remained Wren's loyal supporter to the end, and when Wren was dismissed, Hawksmoor lost his post with the Royal Works as well. By that time he was already working in partnership with Sir John Vanbrugh on such major undertakings as Blenheim Palace and Castle Howard. He succeeded to Wren's post of Surveyor of Westminster Abbey, where he designed and initiated the building of the twin west towers, thereby ending the 500 years it took to complete the building. He died on 25 March 1736 from 'gout in the stomach'. He was Wren's most unusual disciple and one of England's greatest architects.

And then there was Robert Hooke. Three years younger than Wren, he too had been at school at Westminster, and the two young men had probably known each other at Oxford, for they were part of the same scientific circle. Like Wren, Hooke was slight and delicate in person, and became rather bent from intensive study. In 1662 he was appointed curator of experiments to the Royal Society; lifelong tenure was given with the post from 1665, as well as a salary of £30 a year and apartments in Gresham College, one of the few buildings to be spared by the Fire. After that disaster Hooke, like Wren, prepared a design for rebuilding the City on idealised lines. It was never realised, but he was appointed one of the City's three Surveyors for the reconstruction.

Hooke never held a post connected with St Paul's, but he, with Wren, designed the Monument, and he was responsible for at least the supervision, and probably to some extent the design, of several of the City churches, for which Wren was in overall charge. Above all,

Fig. 50 Detail of a trumpet-playing cherub designed by Lord Mottistone, who was Surveyor to the Fabric of the post-war Cathedral. It was presented by the Friends of St Paul's to celebrate the 250th anniversary of the completion of the Cathedral in 1710.

Fig. 51 Detail of the Broomesbury stall on the north side of the quire carved by Grinling Gibbons. There are signs of the repair that is needed constantly.

he was Wren's friend and his sounding board: the two could try out ideas on each other. They frequently dined together in a tavern or at Wren's home, where on 1 February 1679 Hooke gave the architect's four-year-old son Christopher 5 shillings, an immense tip for a little boy when a skilled mason was glad to earn 2s. 6d. a day. As he grew older, he became more suspicious, his temper crustier; sporadically, he kept a diary and frequently noted that he had been 'slighted' by someone, occasionally even by Sir Christopher himself. But Wren's temperament was sunny, and the two remained intellectual companions and friends of a sort till Hooke's death in 1703.

The men who did the actual rebuilding were the masons and carpenters, the bricklayers and smiths. Tenders were invited for the stonework, and the two masons Joshua Marshall and Thomas Strong were chosen. Marshall was an obvious – and excellent – choice. Like his father, Edward, he was Master Mason to the Crown in the Royal Works; he was experienced, of complete integrity, and a most competent organiser and businessman. The elder Marshall must have known Inigo Jones, and he certainly worked under John Webb on The Vyne, a house in Hampshire; he could have passed to his son, and even to Wren, information about Jones's working methods. Such reminiscences would have been reinforced by Edward Arnold, an old carver who had worked on the pre-Fire St Paul's, under Jones; in March 1697, and again the following year, he was given £5 as a mark of appreciation.

Thomas Strong was a craftsman from a different background. He was the third generation of a Cotswold family of masons who worked the limestone quarries at Taynton,

Fig. 52 From the Deanery, just south-west of the Cathedral, this door was the nearest entrance. The carving on the upper part of the door is by William Kempster.

near Burford. He had been employed on the Sheldonian Theatre in Oxford, and on a range of lodgings at Trinity College, Oxford, designed by Wren. It was Strong who laid the first stone for the new St Paul's. Both he and Marshall died in early middle age, Marshall in 1678 and Strong in 1681.

Although three firms were needed to carry on Marshall's work, when it came to replacing Strong, Wren was more fortunate. Thomas had been the eldest of six brothers, all masons, and he left everything to the fifth of them, Edward. On him Wren relied completely. When Wren sent his son abroad, to see the buildings of Paris and Rome, it was Strong's son, another Edward, who went with him, possibly as a steadying influence. It was old Edward, assisted by young Christopher, who set the final stone on St Paul's lantern, high above the London streets.

Masons were generally paid by the measure: that is, once the work was completed, the Surveyor – it might be Woodroffe or Oliver or a specially trained clerk – would measure it carefully, and payment would be reckoned at an agreed figure for each foot or rod of masonry or carving.

Edward Strong took over more than the work at St Paul's from his brother Thomas. The firm held contracts for three City churches: St Stephen Walbrook, its exquisite dome a forerunner of the greater one above the Cathedral; St Benet Paul's Wharf; and, beside St Paul's, St Augustine Watling Street, which was destroyed in 1944 save for its tower, which is now built into the Cathedral's new choir school, with a fibreglass spire reinstating the original design attributed to Hawksmoor, which had been replaced in 1829. Strong was also mason for St Mildred Bread Street (demolished), St Clement Eastcheap and St Michael Paternoster Royal, the fifteenth-century church that had been the burial place of Lord Mayor Richard Whittington. He also built the steeple to St Vedast Foster Lane, designed by Hawksmoor. When St Paul's was complete, Strong went to work on Blenheim, which a grateful nation had voted to bestow on Queen Anne's victorious general, John Churchill, by then the Duke of Marlborough.

LEFT:
Fig. 54 Queen Anne welcomes her subjects as they climb Ludgate Hill towards the Cathedral. The original statue, by Bird, weathered badly and was replaced by a copy in 1885.

OPPOSITE ABOVE:
Fig. 55 A gatepost finial with decorative urn.

OPPOSITE BELOW:
Fig. 56 The pediment to the south portico was carved by Cibber with a phoenix and the word RESURGAM. Significantly, one of Wren's men found this word carved into a wrecked tombstone when work was first starting on the rebuilding.

In spite of having to resort to lawsuits to get his money, Strong made a fortune and bought property in Hertfordshire, where he lived the life of a country gentleman and wrote a history of his firm. He died in his house in St Albans and was buried in St Peter's Church there; his monument, a wall panel over 8 feet (2.4 m) high, has a broken pediment with a periwigged portrait bust between the two halves, the inscription telling of his life's work and association with Wren.

When working on St Stephen Walbrook, Strong had, on Wren's advice, employed another Cotswold mason, Christopher Kempster, as an assistant. Kempster came from the tiny village of Upton, a few miles west of Burford, and he kept a daybook that reveals much about seventeenth-century working methods. He soon became established in London, where he also worked on St James Garlickhythe and on St Mary Abchurch, another domed church, in which Wren worked out his plans for St Paul's.

Kempster joined the St Paul's team in 1690 and with his partner Ephraim Beauchamp was one of the four teams of masons selected to build the dome. He took the south-eastern quarter; the north-west went to Strong, the north-east to Nathaniel Rawlins, and the south-west to the partnership of the younger Thomas Wise and Thomas Hill. When Wren was asked to undertake the completion of Tom Tower for Christ Church, Oxford, it was Kempster whom he recommended for the work, describing him as 'a very able Man, modest, honest and treatable … I can rely on him'.

Christopher Kempster worked in partnership with his brother William, who carved the font at St Mary Abchurch. It was William who built the south-west tower of St Paul's and was responsible for laying the dramatic and intricate black-and-white marble floor. When cracks appeared in some of the pillars of the crypt, it was William Kempster's men who repaired the damage, Wren insisting that Kempster should remain in charge of the masons at all times, leaving nothing to his foreman. He also carved the cluster of cherubs and triangular pediment for the south-west door into the Cathedral, known as the Dean's Door since it is the nearest to the approach from the Deanery in Carter Lane; the work was so good that Wren awarded him an extra £20 for 'the extraordinary diligence and care used in the said carving and his good performance of the same' (figs 48, 52 and 53).

Christopher Kempster retired to his birthplace, where in 1698 he built himself a house. He was buried in Burford church, and for his memorial his son carved a cherub's head, like those above the windows at St Mary Abchurch. The inscription reads:

He liv'd in perfect love and amity with his dear wife near 60 years, by whom he had 5 sons & 7 daughters, and he worked for Christopher Wren in building the cathedral and dome of St Paul's. He died August 12th 1715, in his 89th year.

The epitaph emphasises the importance of the dome.

Working with the masons were the bricklayers, their achievements unseen but nonetheless vital. The original Master Bricklayer, Thomas Warren, and his successor, John Bridges, both died early, but the third craftsman, Richard Billingshurst, remained a member of the team to the end. He was responsible for not only the brick cone on which the dome and lantern relied for support but also the complex brick vaulting over the nave and aisles.

Craftsmen such as these, trained on the abundance of work resulting from the Fire, would be employed on buildings all over England; for a full generation their experience and wisdom would be passed on to others and so made available through succeeding centuries.

As essential as the masons and bricklayers were the carpenters. From the start the Cathedral was well served by Israel Knowles and John Longland. The latter undertook the

Fig. 57 The pediment of the
west front, with Bird's carving
of the Conversion of St Paul
on the road to Damascus.
Surmounting it is a statue of
St Paul.

carpentry for two of the most spectacular City churches: St Bride's and St Stephen Walbrook. When Knowles died, just as the work on the roof of the quire was beginning, Longland took over the entire responsibility until his own death, only a couple of years before the completion of the fabric. As he grew older, he took as partner Richard Jennings, who had already worked with him on the Cathedral for ten years. Jennings was exceptionally able; for his work on the complex centring, which was also the scaffolding across the void of the dome space, Wren awarded him an extra 50 guineas for 'his skill and extraordinary pains, care and diligence'. Later, when there were accusations of fraud and mismanagement, Jennings defended Sir Christopher most stoutly.

Skilled carpentry shades off into joinery, a craft so precise that it seems an art and does indeed sometimes become one; a further refinement is woodcarving. Wren's first joiner was William Cleere, who, at the beginning of the undertaking, made both the First Model and the Great Model, on which his son Richard did the woodcarving. The Cleeres would have made the templates from which the masons carved the stone mouldings. Before long, more than one firm was needed, and the Cleeres were joined by Roger Davis, John Webb and William Samwell. Three names, however, stand out: Grinling Gibbons, Charles Hopson and Jonathan Maine.

From 1695 to 1697 Gibbons was employed on the woodwork of the quire at St Paul's (fig. 49). He carved sixty-six cherubs' heads, their wings folded beneath their chins, festoons of fruit and flowers, acanthus leaves and two superb stalls for the Bishop and the Lord Mayor, the former undertaken with mitre and palm, the latter with sword and mace. The joinery of the choir stalls was undertaken by Charles Hopson, later to serve as Lord Mayor and to receive a knighthood. Wren described him as a 'very honest, able and ingenious workman' – he had already tried him out at Chelsea Hospital and at Eton College. Hopson was a thoroughly sensible person, well educated, good at figures and reliable. Jonathan Maine was a craftsman of the same sort of integrity. Working chiefly in oak – Gibbons preferred limewood – his carving can best be seen in the Morning Prayer Chapel (now known as St Dunstan's Chapel) at the west end of the north aisle.

Stone sculpture was an essential adornment of the Cathedral, and here two names stand out: Caius Gabriel Cibber and Francis Bird. Cibber was Danish by birth but had trained first in Italy and then in the Netherlands. He arrived in England in the late 1650s and found work with the Stone family of masons in Long Acre, Covent Garden. When Nicholas Stone died in 1667, he set up on his own, eventually becoming 'sculptor in ordinary' to William III. He had been responsible for the relief at the base of the Monument showing Charles II, clad like a Roman soldier but wearing a wig, raising up a personification of London from her own ruins; a beehive, prominent in the foreground, symbolises the industry of her citizens. The modernity of the scaffolding seen behind the King is particularly interesting.

Wren set Cibber to work on the keystones in the arches at the crossing; they were huge – 7 feet (2.1 m) high by 5 feet (1.5 m) across – and show fierce angels bearing the crossed swords of St Paul and other emblems. He also carved the centrepiece of the pediment to the south porch, a phoenix rising from its own ashes – a fitting symbol for the Cathedral – and the one word, *RESURGAM*, which had cheered Wren two decades earlier (fig. 56).

Cibber died in 1700 and was replaced by the young Francis Bird, who had trained in Flanders and in Italy; being an 'excellent footman', he had walked all the way to Rome. He sculpted the welcoming figure of Queen Anne (now replaced) that stood before the Cathedral (fig. 54), the vast, shallow font, the figures that perch on the top of the pediment, a panel with St Paul preaching above the central doorway and the great, dramatic *Conversion of St Paul* filling the pediment above the main portico, for which he was paid £650 (fig. 57).

One of the supreme glories of St Paul's is the ironwork. This was the creation of a French smith, Jean Tijou. His first work in England was the decorative panels in the gardens at Hampton Court, where he established his forge. He signed a contract in June 1691 to make two great iron window frames for the quire; these, floated downriver from Hampton, proved satisfactory, and Tijou undertook much of the internal ironwork: the great gates across the aisles at the approach to the sanctuary, screens around the sanctuary and gates beneath the

organ (fig. 58). The work was extraordinary: fantastic yet disciplined. To carry it out, the master smith moved his forge to near Piccadilly, where great houses were being built but which once, then still within living memory, had been lined with the wild bugloss which grows upon the 'dry ditch banks in Piccadilla', described by the herbalist John Gerard at the end of the sixteenth century. Two English smiths, Thomas Robinson and Thomas Coalburne, applied themselves to the less fanciful work. The copperwork of the ball and cross to surmount the lantern was the work of Andrew Niblett.

The chief plumbers, Joseph Roberts and his son Matthew, had already done the leadwork on seventeen City churches. The plasterwork was in the hands of Henry Doogood and John Grove, who mixed a special plaster with ground oyster shells that Robert Streeter painted to look like stone. There remained only the organ, essential equipment in any great church or cathedral. A competition was held between the two most celebrated organ-builders of the day: 'Father' Bernard Smith, a German, and Renatus Harris, a Frenchman. Smith was chosen, though he was known to be a difficult man to work with. The instrument was to have twenty-one stops and six half-stops, and was to stand high on a screen, in a case specially designed by Wren (and carved by Grinling Gibbons), much to 'Father' Smith's disgust; he was accustomed to designing his own organ-cases.

Behind all these names, supporting them indefatigably, were the labourers. The accounts give some idea of the multiplicity of tasks on which they were employed. They seem almost like the chorus in a Greek play. For July 1686 the record runs:

Laborers removeing & wheeling Rubble Stones from the W. end of the Church up into ye Dome, in Screening Separateing Rubbish that was thrown down from the rubble Stones from the Rubbish, in loading of Timber at Paul's WharFe, melting & running of lead for Cramps, beating & boyling of Plaster to make Cement for Masons etc.
1 [man] at 20d. p. day, 26½ days, 21 at 1s. 6d., 494 days, 12 at 1s. 4d., 299½ days.

Their tasks were of an immense variety, and their work far from unskilled.

One of the most amazing things about the building of St Paul's is the teamwork that was involved over so long a period. Wren had his vision, but he had to make that dream a reality, which meant that he had to hold a large and varied body of men to a common purpose. At times it must have seemed impossible, but he made it work. He is thought of as a scientific genius and a great architect, but he was also a great man, with an understanding of other men and an ability to get more out of them than they thought they had in them.

St Paul's was a costly undertaking in terms of manpower and materials. The rebuilding took thirty-four years. The number of men employed on site varied enormously, but at the height of activity there would have been the best part of 400 men busily at work. The largest number of labourers recorded at any one time was 166, the highest total of skilled masons 118, besides bricklayers, carpenters, joiners, smiths, glaziers, plasterers, painters and plumbers. It was an extraordinary co-operative effort.

It was expensive financially too. Through the Coal Tax all of England made a contribution. Contemporary calculations set the cost at £736,752 2s. 4d., which, with £10,909 7s. 8d. for preliminary works, came to £747,661 10s. 0d. And then there was a final exorbitant £11,202 0s. 6d. for Richard Jones's railings. It was a considerable sum of money.

London, however, rejoiced that work was complete at last. James Wright, an elderly barrister who had been writing poems about St Paul's ever since, as a young man, he had gazed up at the ruin, now summed it up:

How shall I fitly name this matchless pile? What equal epithet can fancy give?
Glory of London, Glory of the Isle! Best of the Best! Double superlative!

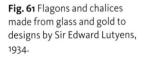

Fig. 61 Flagons and chalices made from glass and gold to designs by Sir Edward Lutyens, 1934.

7

THE HEROES MOVE IN

ONCE THE BUILDING WAS FINISHED, the clergy of St Paul's turned their minds to how best it might be used. It was a huge space, and one quite unlike any other English cathedral. The floor area was some 84,311 square feet (7,832 sq. m). Architecturally, the emphasis was on the vast emptiness under the dome, but liturgical activity was concentrated on the quire, separated from the rest of the building by the organ, its case held aloft on the screen that Wren had designed. It was in the quire that most Sunday and weekday services were celebrated (fig. 62).

Thanksgiving services were held for the Duke of Marlborough's decisive victories over the French, Queen Anne stalwartly dragging her gout-stricken feet up the steps to the west doors. Before one of these occasions, celebrating the victory at Oudenard (23 August 1708), the ridiculous rumour was started that enemies of the realm had loosened the screws holding the dome in place and that the whole centre of the Cathedral would come crashing down during the service, destroying all those within the walls. The idea was absurd – the dome is not held up by screws but is well and truly built, and knitted together with expert carpentry

Fig. 62 Communicants approach the altar in the apse of St Paul's and reverently return to their seats. Jacobus van der Schley's engraving from Bernard Picart's *The Ceremonies and Religious Customs … of the Nations of the World*, 1736.

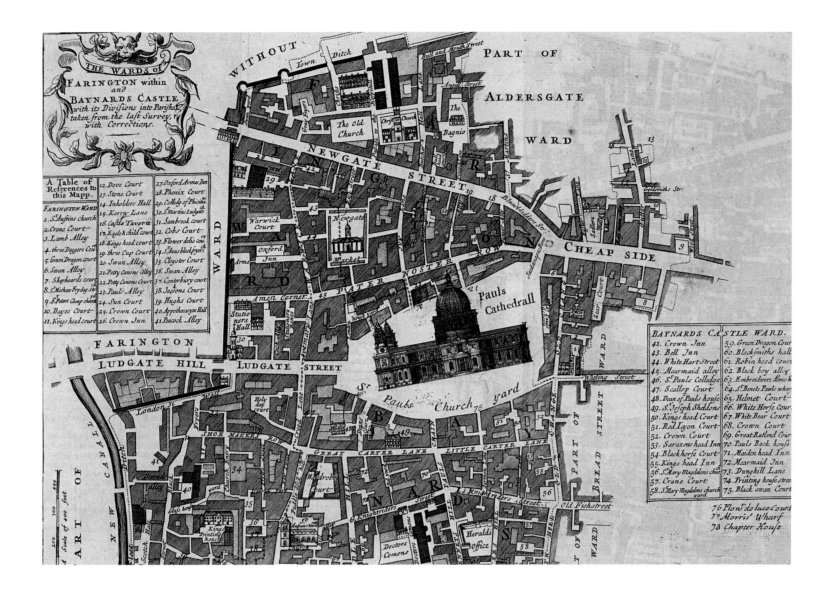

Fig. 63 Richard Bloome's plan of the City, at the centre of which stands St Paul's. The ceremonial route was up Ludgate Hill to the main, west entrance to the Cathedral.

and bricklaying. The Queen ignored the stories and attended as arranged; everything passed off satisfactorily.

Other thanksgivings were held uninterrupted in 1709 for victory at the Battle of Malplaquet and on 7 July 1713 for the Peace of Utrecht. There was no false emergency when the accession of George I was celebrated on 20 January 1717. After that, thanksgivings ceased till St George's Day (23 April) 1789, when the whole nation rejoiced that George III had recovered from what was thought to be madness but was in fact porphyria.

In addition to these, there were the regular annual services to fill the Cathedral. The yearly festival for the sons of the clergy was – and is – one such occasion. An association had been formed in 1655 to help provide education for the sons of clergymen deprived of their livings during the Commonwealth period under Cromwell; the sermons were usually printed afterwards. Today daughters as well as sons are assisted, and entire clerical families are helped when there is need.

Then there were special services for the Society for Promoting Christian Knowledge (founded in 1698) and for the Society for the Propagation of the Gospel (founded 1701). These too filled the building, and after these too the sermon was usually published.

But the service that aroused the greatest public interest and sympathy was the one held annually for the Charity School children. The schools were being founded even before the

Reformation, from the early sixteenth century onwards. The children often wore special uniforms; for the peace thanksgiving of 1713 nearly 4,000 of them filled an enormous stand along the Strand and sang hymns as the procession passed. Services for the children began to be held regularly in churches throughout the capital and the country, and in 1782 the first one was held in St Paul's, nowhere else being large enough to hold the throng. Special seating had to be erected in the body of the Cathedral, which made for a good deal of noise and disturbance as well as trouble over storing in the crypt the planking for the seats when not in use. William Blake, in his poem 'Holy Thursday', recorded such a service:

> *T'was on a Holy Thursday, their innocent faces clean,*
> *The children walking two and two, in red and blue and green,*
> *Grey-headed beadles walk'd before, with wands as white as snow,*
> *Till into the high dome of Paul's they like Thames' water flow.*

The composer Joseph Haydn, on a visit to England, recorded in his diary: 'A week before Whitsun, I heard 4,000 children sing in St Paul's Cathedral … No music ever affected me so powerfully in all my life.' Many years later another composer, Hector Berlioz, in London for the Great Exhibition of 1851, was invited to join the adult choir:

OPPOSITE:
Fig. 66 The first monument admitted to the Cathedral – John Howard, philanthropist and prison reformer, by the elder John Bacon.

ABOVE:
Fig. 67 Bas-relief from Bacon's monument; here we can see the reformer ministering to prisoners.

When I got to the organ loft reserved for the choir, composed of men and boys to the number of seventy, I was given a copy of a bass part which they asked me to sing with the rest, also a surplice which I had to put on, so that my black coat should not clash with the white costumes of the rest of the choir. Disguised thus as a cleric, I awaited the performance with a sort of vague emotion, roused by the spectacle … I was deeply stirred when, the six thousand five hundred little singers being seated, the ceremony began. After a chant on the organ, there burst forth in gigantic unison the first hymn sung by this unique choir: 'All people that on earth do dwell' … [I] managed to take my part in the psalms which were next chanted by the professional choir. Boyce's Te Deum … a piece without character, calmed me down.

The children's services continued till 1872, by which time the numbers were too great to be managed, even in St Paul's.

Music had, from the earliest centuries, been an essential part of Cathedral life. Thomas Morley, who wrote madrigals, was a Vicar Choral; John Barnard, a minor canon, had produced a collection of sacred music in 1641, just before the outbreak of the Civil War; and an authoritative collection of anthems was begun by Maurice Greene, organist of St Paul's.

OPPOSITE:

Fig. 68 Samuel Johnson's monument, carved by the elder John Bacon. Money to erect a statue to the great lexicographer was raised by his friends and by public subscription.

He died before the work was complete, but it was taken up by his friend William Boyce and is still in use today, despite what Berlioz may have felt.

During Greene's earlier years as organist he often received visits from Handel, who delighted to play upon the Cathedral's fine instrument, one of the few in England with a set of pedals. After the great building was shut up for the night, Greene would work the bellows, and Handel, stripped to his shirt in summer, would play away till eight or nine o'clock at night. After that, the pair would make their way to the Queen's Arms coffee house in St Paul's Churchyard and continue to make music there on the harpsichord belonging to the establishment.

The decoration of the interior of the Cathedral was a matter of regular concern. Wren had left it essentially plain. He had intended something more arresting for the interior of the dome, had spoken of mosaic and the bringing over of skilled Italian craftsmen, but he did not make his plans explicit. A competition was held to decide who should have the honour of executing what was currently the most important decorative commission in Europe. The Venetian artist Giovanni Antonio Pellegrini was in England, as were Sebastiano and Marco Ricci, an uncle and nephew also from Venice. Louis Laguerre, godson of Louis XIV, was in London too. But the prize went to James Thornhill (figs 64 and 65).

The English artist respected the physical divisions of the dome, filling each of the eight spaces with a scene from the life of St Paul: the Conversion on the Road to Damascus, the Punishment of the Sorcerer Elymas, the Cure at Lystra, the Conversion of the Gaoler, St Paul Preaching at Athens, the Ephesians Burning Books, St Paul before Agrippa and the Shipwreck at Malta. The paintings are in grisaille, picked out in gold; they may not be exactly what Wren had had in mind, but they are wholly in sympathy with his restrained, almost monochrome, decoration of the interior. A magnificent series of engravings was published showing the detail of the works.

In December 1768 the Royal Academy was founded, under the direct patronage of the King, George III. The President was Sir Joshua Reynolds, who made his fortune from portrait painting but who yearned to produce and to encourage vast historical canvases and murals. The unadorned walls of the Cathedral were enticing, and it was proposed that a team consisting of Reynolds, Benjamin West, James Barry, Angelica Kauffmann, Nathaniel Dance and Giovanni Cipriani should adorn the walls with paintings of biblical subjects. A petition was even presented to the King. But Richard Terrick, Bishop of London, refused to entertain the idea: 'While I live and have the power, I will never suffer the doors of Metropolitan Cathedral to be opened for the introduction of Popery.'

In this he was following the example of his predecessor, Bishop Richard Osbaldeston, who, when petitioned to admit to the Cathedral the statue of a previous Lord Mayor, declared that, if Sir Christopher had intended there to be statues, then he would have designed some. St Paul's remained more or less as Wren had meant it to be.

Before the end of the eighteenth century this restraint was abandoned. Westminster Abbey was already overcrowded with marble memorials. In the spring of 1790 it was decided to erect a monument to John Howard, the son of a wealthy upholsterer. On a voyage to Portugal in 1756 his ship was captured by a French privateer and the crew and passengers imprisoned; they suffered great hardship before their release. Howard decided to dedicate the rest of his life and his fortune to the reform of prisons, and his achievements were such that his supporters opened a subscription during his lifetime to raise a monument to him. Howard himself disapproved of the idea so strongly that it was dropped, but after his death in 1780 his admirers came together again, the Academician John Bacon was selected as sculptor, and the Dean and Chapter agreed that it should stand in St Paul's, the Bishop raising no objection even though Howard was a Nonconformist.

ABOVE:

Fig. 69 Sir Joshua Reynolds, first President of the Royal Academy, the work of John Flaxman.

On 19 May 1791 the Howardian committee – seven Royal Academicians, Canon Jeffreys and Canon Farmer for the Cathedral, and the sculptor – met at St Paul's and decided on a site in the south-east corner under the dome. The price was fixed at 1,800 guineas. It was intended that the sculpture should consist of two figures, resembling, perhaps, Bacon's very moving monument to Thomas Guy in the chapel of Guy's Hospital, which was one of the sculptor's most successful works. It shows the founder of the hospital, dressed as he would have been in life, raising a desperately ill man by the hand to lead him to the hospital, which appears in low relief in the background (figs 66 and 67).

Once one statue was to be admitted, another would follow. Sir Joshua Reynolds won agreement that a memorial to his friend the great writer Samuel Johnson, compiler of one of the earliest English dictionaries, should stand opposite Howard on the north side. Johnson was to be represented in a toga leaning against a pillar; the sculptor, John Bacon, explained the significance of the pose: 'By making him lean against a column, I suggest the firmness of his mind, as well as the stability of his maxims' (fig. 68).

Reynolds must have bargained hard, and Bacon must have been anxious to please the elderly President, for the price was at first fixed at £600, although in the end Bacon was paid £927 13s. 6d. But perhaps because Reynolds feared that the two characters originally planned

Fig. 70 Thomas Banks's monument to George Blagdon Westcott who captained the *Majestic* at the Battle of the Nile is at the north end of the south aisle.

Fig. 71 The bas-relief on the left-hand side of the plinth shows the French flagship *L'Orient* exploding – a remarkable feat of carving.

for the Howard monument would make it seem more important than the sole figure of Johnson, it was now decided that the original design should be put on one side and a single figure of Howard in a Greek chiton and sandals substituted for it. Bacon protested but was overruled; the price for the Howard memorial was reduced to 1,300 guineas.

Johnson stands, rugged and solid; apart from the garb, the figure conveys the spirit of the man. Howard's memorial is less appealing to the modern eye. The tunic and draperies detract from the reformer's significance; the huge key in his hand made one nineteenth-century visitor assume that he was looking at a statue of St Peter, with St Paul standing near by. Bacon was never happy with it, and put all his undoubted skill into the bas-relief on the pedestal, where Howard, here also in classical draperies, ministers to poor wretches in prison while an attendant brings food and drink and – in the very lowest relief – the gaoler at the head of a flight of steps mercifully unlocks the door.

Time and again, the carving on the pedestal is the key to the real meaning of a monument. The conventions of the day might demand togas and chitons, and drapery and classical poses; the bas-relief tells the story.

Howard and Johnson were soon joined by similarly heroic figures in memory of Sir William Jones and of Reynolds. Jones, an Orientalist and barrister, became Judge of the High Court in Calcutta; his studies of Hindu and Arabic literature and law were profound, and the bas-relief on the memorial in the south transept, once again by Bacon, is filled with Oriental figures, including a small and charming Indian goddess. Sir Joshua's monument, in the north-west corner of the crossing, was carved by John Flaxman, perhaps the most important of the next generation of sculptors. It is a dignified work; the artist leans against a pedestal on which is carved a cameo portrait of Michelangelo; he clasps a stout, well-bound volume, presumably an edition of his own *Discourses on Art* (fig. 69). The acoustics in St Paul's are notoriously difficult, and the tradition has grown up that the preacher should always 'speak to Sir Joshua'.

Those four larger than life-size figures opened the floodgates for what was to come. In 1793 Revolutionary France declared war on England. The range of ensuing wars was astonishing – not simply right across the European land mass, from Portugal to the depths of Russia and from Copenhagen to Italy, but also across the oceans, to Egypt, the West Indies, America, Canada, Ceylon and Nepal – and throughout the turmoil of the next twenty-two years the government voted and paid for no fewer than thirty-three marble memorials to heroes of the extended struggle. Two of the sculptures are in Westminster Abbey, the rest in St Paul's, which became thereby a Valhalla to the men who fought, and for the most part died, in the wars against France and Napoleon. In all, government patronage amounted to £100,000.

Two of the most eye-catching in St Paul's stand in the south aisle. They are to Captain Richard Burges and to Captain George Westcott; both are the work of Thomas Banks, whose seven years of study in Italy had been at the expense of the Royal Academy. Burges, a handsome figure standing beside a canon and a most realistic coil of rope, is clad in nothing but a cloak; he receives a sword from a winged Victory. He fell commanding the *Ardent* on 11 September 1797 at the Battle of Camperdowne, off the Dutch coast, an engagement that also resulted in the death of Viscount Duncan, whose monument was carved by Sir Richard Westmacott.

Banks's tribute to Westcott is ungainly. Victory, laurel crown in hand, staggers as she supports the falling body of the captain of the *Majestic*. His figure, wearing a tunic, gives no impression of the man himself, who died in one of Nelson's bloodiest engagements, the Battle of the Nile, on 1 August 1798. That is illustrated in the reliefs on the pedestal. The central panel, conventionally enough, shows Neptune leaning against a sphinx with a palm tree near by, but that to the left-hand side is an astonishing representation of the French flagship *L'Orient* exploding: a proper tribute to the man commemorated, and to the sculptor's skill (figs 70 and 71).

Fig. 72 Sir Richard
Westmacott's monument to
Admiral Lord Collingwood,
Nelson's friend and second-in-
command.

Often, in the plethora of symbolic figures, garlands and victorious wreaths, it is the inscription that first demands attention, as with Captain Robert Faulknor's monument in the north transept. Following family tradition, Faulknor went to naval college at eleven and to sea at fourteen. In action against the French in the early years of the war, his frigate *Blanche* engaged *La Pique*, and when the latter's bowsprit swung athwart his own vessel, Faulknor seized it and lashed it to the capstan, thereby rendering *Blanche*'s fire more deadly; he himself was killed a moment afterwards. It is worth standing still to read the long inscription. His monument, the work of John Charles Felix Rossi, was not carved till ten years later; seated Neptune catches the hero's falling body while Victory bestows a wreath. Public opinion was quicker to react to Faulknor's extraordinary feat, for a dramatic interlude was promptly put on at Covent Garden with the battle as the climax.

Another admiral who, like the others, might have smiled at the character of his tribute is Cuthbert, Lord Collingwood (figs 72–4). It was he who took command at Trafalgar when Nelson, his friend as well as his commander, was killed. Collingwood remained at sea, pursuing his duty for the next five years, and died aboard his flagship, *Ville de Paris*, on 7 March 1810. His body was brought back to England, and Westmacott, in his monument to Collingwood in the south transept, shows the admiral lying on the deck of a man-of-war,

Fig. 73 Along the gunwale are
four little putti representing
the progress of navigation.
One explores the oceans
guided by the stars.

Fig. 74 Another putto playfully
climbs up Neptune's arm.

OPPOSITE:
Fig. 75 There is an extraordinary degree of realism in Westmacott's memorial to Lieutenant-General Sir Ralph Abercromby. He died in 1801 during the Egyptian campaign.

ABOVE:
Fig. 76 The younger John Bacon's monument to General Sir John Moore, who was killed at Corunna in Spain in 1809. The realistically furled standard gives height to the group.

shrouded in colours won from the enemy, his hands still clasping a sword. Kneeling Fame leans over him; Neptune contemplates the hero. Along the gunwale are a series of little scenes in relief representing the progress of navigation: the genius of man explores the oceans with the stars for a guide; he uses the magnetic compass and forges the instruments of war.

After so much symbolism it is something of a change to look at another sculpture by Westmacott in the south transept: the monument to Lieutenant-General Sir Ralph Abercromby, who was mortally wounded during the Egyptian campaign and died on 28 March 1801. It shows the general, in uniform, falling from his horse into the arms of a kilted Highland soldier. Sphinxes flank the main group, which is carved with an impressive freedom and liveliness (fig. 75).

The same verisimilitude appears in Sir John Moore's memorial, again in the south transept, by the younger John Bacon, son of the man responsible for the first three statues to be admitted into the Cathedral. Moore died at Corunna on 16 January 1809, during the first Peninsular campaign. His body, properly uniformed, is being lowered into the tomb by an angel and a half-naked man, representing Victory and Valour, while the genius of Spain in the guise of a cherub mournfully holds a flag aloft (fig. 76).

Fig. 77 Nelson's memorial carved by John Flaxman. The missing arm is disguised by a fur cloak, the gift of the Tsar of Russia; the sculptor's skill conveys the sightlessness of the left eye.

ABOVE:
Fig. 78 Glass painting in the Cathedral library of Nelson's coffin being conveyed up the Thames, from Greenwich to Whitehall, by members of the crew of HMS *Victory*.

At first glance John Flaxman's memorial to Nelson in the south transept seems to be yet another group of symbolic figures clustered around a pedestal supporting a statue. Examined more closely, it is clear that Britannia is telling two young naval cadets or schoolboys about Nelson's victories, while the figure of the admiral conveys his power of leadership; opposite, the British lion growls menacingly (fig. 77).

The admiral's body, preserved in spirits, was brought back to England after his death at the Battle of Trafalgar on 21 October 1805. It lay in state at Greenwich and was then rowed up the Thames by sixteen of the crew of the *Victory* to the Admiralty in Whitehall, whence, after another pause, it was brought to St Paul's on an elaborate funeral car on 9 January 1806. The coffin was made from the mainmast of *L'Orient* (shown exploding on Westcott's monument) (fig. 78).

Nelson was interred with the utmost ceremony, in a service lasting four hours. His body rests in a magnificent sarcophagus originally commissioned by Cardinal Wolsey from Benedetto da Rovezzano. When the cardinal fell from power in 1529, Henry VIII seized the sarcophagus, possibly intending it for his own occupation, but it lay unused till it was deemed a worthy resting place for England's greatest naval hero (fig. 79).

Two years after Nelson's death, the Parthenon marbles, brought to safety from Athens by the Earl of Elgin, were put on view in London. They had a profound influence on art in England, which can be seen, though perhaps indirectly, in Francis Chantrey's dramatic relief panels to three heroes of the Peninsular War: Major General Daniel Hoghton, Major General Bernard Bowes and Colonel Henry Cadogan (the first two in the north transept, the last in the south transept). Each represents a leader dying in action; each gets its effect by repetition:

OPPOSITE:
Fig. 79 Nelson's tomb, raised high in the middle of the crypt, is a startling and sombre object, a sarcophagus carved in the early sixteenth century by Benedetto da Rovezzano. The casket is surmounted by a viscount's coronet.

ABOVE:
Fig. 80 The influence of the Elgin marbles, newly arrived in London, is evident in the monument to Sir William Ponsonby, who died at the Battle of Waterloo. The monument was designed by William Theed and executed by Edward Baily.

parallel lines of musket muzzles or fixed bayonets, ranks of troops suggested by outlines of their headgear. Chantrey, a self-taught sculptor like Bacon, had looked closely at the Parthenon frieze.

The influence of the free-standing sculpture from the Parthenon is evident in Sir William Ponsonby's memorial. As Ponsonby led a troop of cavalry at the Battle of Waterloo, his horse stumbled and he was ridden down by French lancers. The large monument, now in the crypt, was designed by William Theed and executed by Edward Baily; it shows the naked, recumbent warrior reclining against the fallen horse and reaching up for a wreath from winged Victory. The horse's head owes much to the Parthenon sculpture, but the result is not happy (fig. 80).

There are unexpected delights to be found among this group of early nineteenth-century sculptures. The dying Sir Isaac Brock, who fell at Queenstown in Canada, is regarded sympathetically by a splendid North American Indian (south transept); Captain George Hardinge, who died of wounds received in a victorious action off the coast of Ceylon on 8 March 1808, has a contemplative Indian nursing the British colours (south transept); Generals Pakenham and Gibbs, who died in 1815 in an attack on New Orleans, stand shoulder to shoulder (south transept); Captain George Duff, another casualty of Trafalgar, is mourned by a fine figure of an able seaman (crypt).

By the time the wars ended with the Battle of Waterloo in 1815, and the last figures were completed in the 1830s, St Paul's rivalled Westminster Abbey as the shrine to those who had upheld the nation, whether in peace or in war. These figures hold the nation's memory.

8

THE VICTORIAN CATHEDRAL

ONCE THE WARS WITH FRANCE WERE OVER, Britain turned to industrial expansion and to reform. Despite opposition, the Reform Act, giving the vote to a far wider range of electors, was passed in 1832. One of its principal supporters was a clergyman, Sydney Smith, who in 1831 was appointed a canon of St Paul's. Although by then aged sixty, Smith was still vigorous, active and superbly witty. Almost twenty years earlier, he had been a founder of the *Edinburgh Review*, a journal of humane and liberal principles. He campaigned against slavery, transportation, harsh prisons and the Game Laws, and urged Church reform and Catholic emancipation as well as supporting the Reform Bills of 1831 and 1832.

In 1828 Charles James Blomfield had become Bishop of London; he stood on Ludgate Hill, looking upwards and said: 'I look at that great Cathedral and think of its large revenues and ask myself, what good is it doing to this great city, and I feel compelled to answer nothing to a single soul in it.' With men such as these, and with Edward Copleston as Dean and William Hale as Archdeacon, there were going to be changes.

The most obvious problem was the near impossibility of keeping so large a building clean and heated. Since 1727 eleven successive Deans had also been diocesan bishops; the intention was that the revenues of St Paul's, which, though not large, were adequate, should help to fund under-endowed provincial sees. Inevitably, the Deans' attentions and energies were divided. Similarly, most of the clergy held livings elsewhere.

Sydney Smith took over the accounts and kept them with great good humour but with the utmost strictness. Archdeacon Hale, with C. R. Cockerell as Surveyor to the Fabric, replaced all broken windows in the crypt, installed gas lighting, had the walls and monuments cleaned and organised a wagon of hot coals to be dragged around to try to take the chill off the interior. It did not make much difference; 'the only real way of doing it is warm the county of Middlesex', Canon Smith told him. In the end, huge stoves were installed in the crypt and gratings were opened in the floor of the nave, which made for some improvement.

Edward Copleston, though also Bishop of Llandaff, was assiduous in his duties as Dean, scarcely ever missing a meeting of the Chapter. When he died in 1849, he was succeeded first by Henry Hart Milman, who wrote an excellent history of St Paul's, and then, some while later, by Robert Gregory, who had come to the Cathedral as a canon in 1868. For fifteen years he had been vicar of St Mary-the-Less at Lambeth. It was a poor and overcrowded area, and the vicar was scarcely better off than his parishioners. When he heard of his appointment, his first thought was for his family: 'Now we can get a rocking-horse for the little children.' But although he felt tenderly for the young, for the forty-three years that he served the

Fig. 81 This room above the south aisle has been the theological working library of St Paul's since 1720. Much of the woodwork is by Jonathan Maine. A portrait of Sydney Smith dominates the chimney-breast at gallery level, and one of Bishop Compton is over the fireplace. Pierce's bust of Wren sits on the Librarian's desk.

Cathedral he was a rigid disciplinarian, insisting on punctual attendance at services and proper observance of due forms and ceremonies.

Far-reaching changes were beginning to be made by the middle of the nineteenth century. Church property and estates were being vested in the hands of the Ecclesiastical Commissioners in return for a fixed income, and an Act of July 1868 meant that in future St Paul's would be largely dependent on an allowance from the Commissioners. The only property that was retained was the Manor of Tillingham, in Essex, which had belonged to the Cathedral since before the Norman Conquest.

Dean Milman and Dean Gregory had an unlikely supporter in Miss Maria Hackett. A well-to-do unmarried lady, she lived with her uncle in Crosby Square, just off Bishopsgate. In 1810 a young cousin, Henry Wintle, became a chorister at St Paul's, and Maria undertook responsibility for him. She soon realised that the choirboys needed a champion. Apart from the study of music, they received little or no education and all too often were simply left to their own devices or to idleness. Originally the children of the choir had formed part of the Dean's household and had boarded with the almoner, but funds had become inadequate; they now lived at home, which might entail a long, unsupervised journey, especially when their services had been hired out for an evening concert. No provision was made for the boys' continuing education after their voices had broken.

Miss Hackett began to write letters and to waylay and lecture the clergy, and also presented a petition in Chancery on the choristers' behalf. It was not till Gregory was appointed a canon that matters began to improve; eventually a choir school was built in Carter Lane, and the boys began to be properly looked after. Miss Hackett took to touring cathedral cities to inspect and advise on the condition of the choristers. Her determination, though no

LEFT:
Fig. 82 Memorial to Sir Arthur Wellesley Torrens, who died at the Battle of Inkermann in the Crimean War. The marble relief panel shows him on horseback in the midst of the fighting; it is the north aisle.

ABOVE:
Fig. 83 Miss Maria Hackett, the chiorboys champion. A silhouette of her in her youth.

OPPOSITE:
Fig. 84 Memorial to J. M. W. Turner, RA, by Patrick McDowell, RA. Easy to overlook among the admirals and generals in the south transept, the alert face and purposeful hand holding a palette are carved most realistically.

doubt very trying to complacent clerics, made life much better for many children. She was also the prime mover in saving from demolition Crosby Hall, a superb fifteenth-century building grown derelict, and in its transfer to and rebuilding in Chelsea.

Throughout the nineteenth century the Cathedral was fortunate in its organists. Thomas Attwood had been a favourite pupil of Mozart, with whom he studied in Vienna. He returned to England in 1796 to join St Paul's, where he stayed for the rest of his life. In old age he recognised the genius of Mendelssohn and invited him to play at the Cathedral. One Sunday afternoon in 1829 the young virtuoso played on after the service, and the congregation lingered to hear him so that the virgers could not close the building. In desperation, in the middle of a Bach fugue, they let the air out of the organ and in the silence cleared the throng.

Attwood was succeeded by John Goss, a talented and ingenious musician. On one occasion all the choir were absent save for one tenor and one bass, and they were due to give the Hallelujah Chorus from Handel's *Messiah*. The wretched pair sent word up to Goss in the organ loft. 'Do your best', said he, 'and I will do the rest with the organ'; and he did.

When the aged Duke of Wellington died in 1852, thirty-seven years after the Battle of Waterloo, Goss played at his funeral, composing for it two anthems and a dirge, or funeral lament. That was one of the most extraordinary services ever to take place in St Paul's. Seating had to be erected for 13,000 people. Thousands of yards of black cloth were provided to exclude all natural light; though not entirely successful, the effect was sombre in the extreme.

Wellington's memorial, which stands in the middle of the north aisle of the nave, is the work of Alfred Stevens. It is enormous, towering up to the vaulting above and at variance with the earlier marble tributes to those who had fought beside the Duke. It is one of the most astonishing works of sculpture produced in Britain during the nineteenth century (fig. 86).

Stevens was the son of a Dorset house painter. His natural talent was so extraordinary

Fig. 85 At the western end of the north aisle is Sir Edgar Boehm's memorial to General George Gordon who fell at the siege of Khartoum, 1885.

that the Rector of Blandford Forum, the Hon. and Revd Samuel Best, sent him to Italy, where he studied for nine years, part of the time as a student of the celebrated Danish sculptor Bertel Thorwaldsen. Five years after Wellington's death, a competition was held to choose a sculptor for the Duke's tomb monument. Stevens was the winner.

The monument, architectural in scale, was designed in three stages: an effigy of Wellington lying on a sarcophagus and under a canopy, above which two supremely dramatic groups are poised: Truth plucking out the tongue of Falsehood and Valour spurning Cowardice. A third storey supports an equestrian statue of the Duke.

The execution of the monument was protracted and stormy. The concept was elaborate, Stevens had confidently underestimated how much time and effort would be needed, and successive governments were harsh taskmasters. The competition rules had laid down that £20,000 was the price limit for the work; Stevens was persuaded – or induced – to accept £14,000. Then he was required to produce a full-scale model, an immense labour in itself. Stevens toiled at it, often fitfully for his was a dilatory nature, for eighteen years; civil servants goaded him. Then, unexpectedly, he died. The work was completed, save for the equestrian statue, by his pupils and installed in the north-west chapel, which it completely filled. In 1894 it was moved to its present position under the centre arch of the north arcade of the nave; in 1903 John Tweed restored the plaster model for the horse and rider, which was cast in bronze and put in position in 1912. The whole work had taken nearly fifty-six years, rather longer than it took for Wren to build the entire Cathedral.

For the rest of the century, far more is known about the daily and domestic workings of St Paul's, for the staff had been joined by Virger Robert Green. He served from 1852 till 1899, and he kept a detailed diary of all that happened.

In 1859 it was decided to enlarge and improve the organ. For the work to be carried out, it was necessary to dismantle the instrument. At the same time, the screen across the quire was removed and everyone was thrilled with the vista this opened up. The organ was first reinstalled on the north side of the quire and then, later, divided between the two halves of the quire, Wren's case being adapted to fit the new arrangement. Another, smaller, organ was installed in the west gallery. The opening up of the quire into the dome and nave areas meant that a much larger group of choristers was needed. By 1874 there were forty boys in the choir school.

Two years earlier, the capacity of St Paul's had been tested once again. Seating for 14,000 was needed for a thanksgiving service on 27 February 1872 for the recovery of the Prince of Wales from typhoid, the disease that had killed his father, Prince Albert, just over a decade earlier. Queen Victoria came out of her self-imposed seclusion for the occasion and drove with her son and daughter-in-law, Princess Alexandra, to the Cathedral. John Goss composed an anthem and a *Te Deum*, for which he was knighted. He used to say that he believed he was the only knight resident in Brixton. He retired later that year and lived on happily, receiving an honorary doctorate from Cambridge, a distinction that was also bestowed at the ceremony on his former pupil Arthur Sullivan. A white marble panel was

unveiled to him in the crypt, carved by Hamo Thornycroft, with five surpliced choirboys and the opening bars of Goss's own anthem 'If we believe that Jesus died', which had been sung at his funeral. His memorial is near to the plaque to Miss Hackett's memory.

In Goss's place came John Stainer, a contemporary and friend of Sullivan. The composition for which he is best remembered is *The Crucifixion*, still performed regularly in St Paul's. On retiring at last in 1888, owing to failing eyesight, he too was knighted.

With the opening up of the central vista, the clergy of St Paul's turned their minds again to the decoration of the interior. In 1872 an approach was made to William Burges to introduce colour into the quire and dome areas. It was a strange choice of adviser. A devotee of the High Gothic style who regarded Wren's churches as 'abominations', Burges recommended covering all the internal walls with thin layers of highly coloured marble. Rather fortunately, even by his own estimate the cost was prohibitive. Then G. F. Bodley was approached to design a new high altar to provide a more positive focus. This he did, in multi-coloured marbles with a Crucifixion scene as its centre; it was the first time since the

Reformation that such a subject had been represented in the Cathedral. Although impressive in its own right, it could hardly be said to have been in harmony with Wren's building.

The architect's original suggestion of mosaic work was then revived, though not in place of Thornhill's paintings. A first essay was made in the spandrels of the great central arches of the dome. Alfred Stevens was commissioned to make designs for the prophets Isaiah (fig. 89), Jeremiah, Ezekiel and Daniel. Unfortunately he completed only the first, and the remaining three were the rather less decisive work of W. E. F. Britten. George Frederic Watts was then asked to provide the four Evangelists, Matthew, Mark, Luke and John. All eight designs were executed in flat, smooth mosaic.

In 1891 William Richmond was approached about mosaics for the whole eastern part of the Cathedral. Work began almost immediately. Instead of the polished decorations already executed, Richmond decided on a more rugged method. Each rough-cut tessera was set individually by hand, so that the light reflects from it, giving a lively, seemingly changing surface. There was immense excitement over the work as it progressed.

The three saucer-domes over the vault of the quire take their theme from the *Benedicite* ('O all ye works of the Lord, praise ye the Lord'). In the westernmost dome are animals of every kind; in the centre are fishes, with magnificent whales spouting water (fig. 94); and in the east swoop the birds of the air (fig. 93). In the spandrels between the little domes, angels with upraised arms spread their wings (fig. 90). In the eastern apse the figure of Christ sits in majesty on a rainbow, raising his hands in blessing, flanked by recording angels, cherubim and seraphim (fig. 92).

The decoration of the north and south aisles is equally elaborate – much thought and study must have gone into the choice of subjects and texts. Particularly effective are the Delphic and Persian Sibyls at clerestory level (the upper level of windows) on the north side of the quire; the rectangular panels above the organ showing Adam caressing a lion and lioness, and Eve with a tiger and tigress; and the Annunciation scene high above the easternmost arch.

While the work was still in progress, it was calculated that 12 tons of special cement and 6,750,000 tesserae had already been used. The glass was made, and the mosaics installed, by teams of workmen trained by Messrs Powell of Whitefriars. The money was raised by public subscription, from private donors and from four of the City Livery Companies: the Merchant Taylors, the Mercers, the Goldsmiths and the Grocers, who paid for the *Crucifixion*, the *Entombment*, the *Resurrection* and the *Ascension* in the central quarter-domes. The work was finished in 1907. There was talk of extending it, but money had run out, public

BELOW:
Fig. 90 Mosaic decoration in the crossing: in a spandrel an angel soars upwards.

VOLATILE SVB FIRMAMENTO ET

POPULUS QVI AMBVL... ...T IN TE... ...EBRIS VIDIT

OPPOSITE:
Fig. 92 The full glory of the quire mosaic, representing the Creation. In the apse, The Risen Christ in Glory; in the domes, the birds in the air, the beasts in the fields, and the fish in the sea.

ABOVE:
Fig. 93 Quire mosaic: the birds of the air rejoice in full song.

OVERLEAF:
Fig. 94 Quire mosaic: the fishes abound in the oceans, whales spouting joyously.

opinion was divided about it, and then the First World War came and no more was done. The decorations give the eastern arm a radiance in which it would not otherwise rejoice.

At the end of the century, on 22 June 1897, a special service was held for Queen Victoria's Diamond Jubilee (fig. 95). The Queen, who at her coronation in Westminster Abbey had lightly sprung up to help the elderly Archbishop Howley when he stumbled on the steps, was now too old and infirm to drag herself up to the western doors, so stands were erected around the top of Ludgate Hill, and the Queen sat in her carriage while the service was held outside. Fortunately, the weather was fine. The Lambeth Conference was happening at the time, and more than a hundred bishops from all over the world stood on the Cathedral steps. The clergy of St Paul's all wore their copes, which added to the colourfulness of the occasion.

The Queen, who had always hoped to see in the new century, died on 22 January 1901, and a memorial service was held for her in St Paul's. The long Victorian epoch had ended.

Fig. 95 Queen Victoria's Diamond Jubilee, 1897. More than a hundred clergy assembled on the steps of the cathedral, backed by choirs and musicians. The Queen sat attentively in her carriage; Queen Anne's statue bore witness to royal support through the centuries.

9

PERIL AND SURVIVAL

O N 5 JUNE 1908 St Paul's received a great and extraordinary treasure in the life-
size, third version of *The Light of the World*, by William Holman Hunt (fig. 96). As
a young man, in 1851, Hunt had begun the original painting, now in Keble College,
Oxford; a second, smaller, version is now in Manchester City Art Gallery. The work was
inspired by verse 20 of the third chapter of the Book of Revelation: 'Behold, I stand at the
door and knock; if any man hear my voice, and open the door, I will come to him and will
sup with him, and he with me.' Christ, lantern in hand, is shown knocking at the door of
the heart. The door is overgrown with ivy; it has no handle since it can be opened only from
within. Christ stands waiting, attentive and patient; light streams from the lantern He holds,
and some of the apertures are in the shape of crosses and crescents, indicating that His message is for all the world – not only for those already nominally Christian, but for those of
other faiths as well.

This third version, painted when Hunt was an old man, partially blind and receiving help
from another artist, Edward Hughes, is an extraordinarily powerful and moving work. It was
purchased by the philanthropist Charles Booth, was sent on tour around Canada, Australia,
New Zealand and South Africa, where it was seen by millions of eager viewers, and was
finally presented to St Paul's Cathedral, where it has been an object of contemplation, a
source of comfort and consolation, ever since.

By the early twentieth century, monuments had begun to multiply in the crypt. Wren's
presence drew architects and engineers. Among those either buried or commemorated in St
Paul's are Robert Mylne and John Rennie, the former a Surveyor to the Fabric of the
Cathedral and architect of the original Blackfriars Bridge, the latter the designer of Waterloo
Bridge and Southwark Bridge (both also now replaced); the younger George Dance, one of
the original forty Royal Academicians; C. R. Cockerell, another Surveyor to the Fabric of the
Cathedral; and the architect Sir Edwin Lutyens.

If Westminster Abbey has Poets' Corner, then St Paul's has a special tenderness for
artists. Anthony van Dyck, court painter to Charles I, had been buried in old St Paul's, and
Sir Joshua Reynolds, the first President of the Royal Academy, was interred in Wren's
building in 1792, soon to be joined by other Royal Academicians. Benjamin West, the
American painter who succeeded Sir Joshua as President, Henry Fuseli, John Opie and
James Barry (the only Academician ever to be ejected from that august body), all lie or are

Fig. 96 *The Light of the World.*
In the dark of the night, Christ
holds a lantern. The light from
it streams through crescents
as well as small crosses, to
show that His message is not
only for Christians.

THE
OF THE
LIGHT
WORLD

BEHOLD I STAND AT THE DOOR AND KNOCK IF ANY MAN
HEAR MY VOICE AND OPEN THE DOOR I WILL COME
IN TO HIM AND WILL SVP WITH HIM AND HE WITH ME.

remembered here. Later generations joined them: J. M. W. Turner (fig. 84), John Constable, William Holman Hunt and Randolph Caldecott (fig. 97).

A succession of twelve Presidents of the Royal Academy (all of them knights) are commemorated, from Frederic, Lord Leighton, whose main memorial is upstairs, to John Millais, Edward Poynter, Aston Webb, Frank Dicksee, William Llewellyn, Edwin Landseer, Alfred Munnings, Gerald Kelly, Albert Richardson, Charles Wheeler and Thomas Monnington. Here as well is Edwin Austin Abbey, an American artist who became an Academician and left a substantial sum to the Academy for commissioning large works of art for public places.

There are sculptor knights too: Hamo Thornycroft, Joseph Edgar Boehm, the first artist to be made a baronet, George Frampton, whose *Peter Pan* still delights children in Kensington Gardens, Alfred Gilbert, creator of *Eros* in Piccadilly Circus, and William Reid Dick, whose best work is seen in the ensemble of the Kitchener Memorial (All Souls) Chapel.

One of the most powerful memorials is that to John Singer Sargent, who made his name as a dashing and perceptive society portrait painter but who created works of a different kind too, such as the deeply moving bronze crucifix that his sisters presented to the Cathedral in his memory.

Music is not forgotten. In addition to memorials to Cathedral organists and choristers, there is one to Sir Arthur Sullivan, who composed church music and, with W. S. Gilbert supplying the words, the operettas that have amused his own and succeeding generations.

Turning away from the arts, there is a tablet to Charles Booth, recalling his concern for the 'social industrial and religious condition of the people of London'. Intellectually and spiritually, he keeps company with Sir Stafford Cripps, of whom a half-length bronze statue by Sir Jacob Epstein stands in a niche in the south aisle.

On a grimmer note, war correspondents are remembered too. The doyen of them all, Sir William Russell, who reported on the Crimean War in the 1850s, has a lively bronze bust representing him with pencil and notebook in hand. Seven reporters died in the Sudan between 1883 and 1885, and thirteen in the South African War of 1889 to 1902.

More recently, memorials have begun to be set up to those who died long ago but were not commemorated at the time. William Blake, who died in 1827, was accorded a tablet a century later. John Wyclif, translator of the Bible into English, who died in 1384, was given a plaque in 1986. The funeral in old St Paul's of Sir Philip Sidney, Queen Elizabeth's courtier and poet, who died at Zutphen in 1586, was one of the grandest ever accorded a commoner; he is remembered by a tablet carved by David Kindersley and Lida Lopes Cardozo in 1985. The majority of these memorials are, like many of the earlier ones, remarkable for the excellence of the lettering.

The outbreak of the First World War in August 1914, and the first Zeppelin raid on London in September the following year, aroused fears for the safety of the Cathedral. Canon Alexander and the Surveyor of the Fabric, Mervyn Macartney, organised the first St Paul's Watch; a nightly vigil was kept, voluntarily, by those who loved the Cathedral. Mercifully, no bombs fell on it, though one of Britain's own shells struck the south-east edge of the cornice on 30 September 1917. Armistice was declared on 11 November 1918, and the next day a special thanksgiving service was attended by King George and Queen Mary.

Even before the outbreak of war, fresh dangers had threatened the Cathedral. In 1911 it was proposed that a new bridge be built across the Thames and that, as part of the undertaking, a train tunnel be constructed close to the east end of St Paul's. Evidence collected about the possible ill effects of such a project suggested that there was work to be done within the Cathedral itself. Wren had taken borings and had been most scrupulous in his positioning of the huge building in relation to the subsoil, but even in his day the enormous weight had

Fig. 97 Sir Alfred Gilbert's memorial to the artist Randolph Caldecott is in the crypt. A mourning child holds a medallion bearing the artist's head in relief.

Fig. 98 Florence Nightingale ministers tenderly to a wounded soldier. Her determination and capacity for organisation transformed the whole concept of nursing. The relief was sculpted by the Academician A. G. Walker and is in the crypt.

BELOW:
Fig. 99 The Chapel of All Souls, set aside for private prayer, contains Sir William Reid Dick's memorial to Earl Kitchener who relieved the siege of Khartoum. Thirty-one years later, he was lost when HMS *Hampshire* sank off the coast of Orkney.

inevitably compressed the clay beneath it, and as early as 1694 repairs had been needed to the piers supporting the dome. This reinforcement had been supplemented by the girdling of the dome itself with a massive iron chain forged by Thomas Coalburne and Thomas Robinson.

Now more work was needed, and the Canon Treasurer, S. A. Alexander, undertook the raising of three substantial public appeals, in 1914, 1922 and 1925. Cement was injected into the interiors of the main piers, masonry was renewed or replaced, cramps of rust-resistant steel were inserted, and another chain was added to the outer drum of the dome. Wren's use of metal cramps and ties had been innovative; being aware of possible deterioration, he had for the most part made sure that the iron was not exposed to the atmosphere, but, where protection was not possible, decay had followed. From 1925 to 1930 it was necessary to close off parts of the Cathedral so that the work might be carried out uninterrupted. When it was complete, the whole central structure, and in particular the piers carrying the weight of the dome, were restored. There were those, including William Ralph Inge, the Dean, who felt that Canon Alexander's anxieties were unnecessary; but, in view of what was to come, the canon may be considered the Cathedral's saviour. He held his appointment from 1909 till his death in 1948 and, deservedly, was buried in the crypt.

In 1934 Walter Robert Matthews became Dean, and it became his responsibility to protect St Paul's throughout the Second World War. The danger in 1939 was far more real

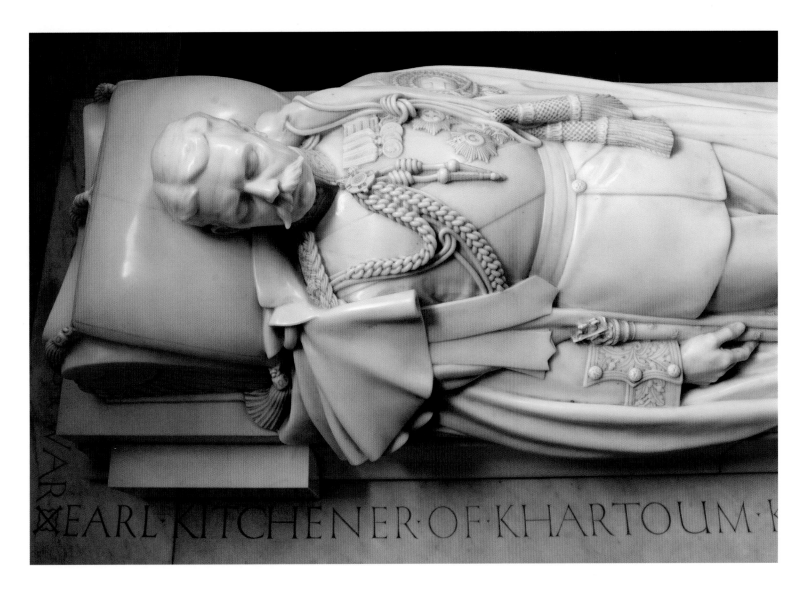

EARL·KITCHENER·OF·KHARTOUM·K

Fig. 100 St Paul's in the Blitz. This celebrated photograph, taken on the night of 29 December 1940, came to symbolise the steadfast endurance of St Paul's – and of London – throughout the ordeal.

than it had been between 1914 and 1918. Six months before the outbreak of war plans had been laid, and once again a band of more than sixty volunteers, the St Paul's Watch, had been recruited, led by the Surveyor, Godfrey Allen, who had been appointed in 1931. Movable treasures were evacuated or carried to the comparative safety of the crypt; Dean Matthews slept, when he could, beside the sandbag-covered monument of his predecessor John Donne.

Throughout the war services continued, as near as possible to normal arrangements, though the choir school was evacuated to Truro, in the west country, where, in the cathedral, the boys continued to sing. Every Christmas, King George VI sent as usual two tall trees to St Paul's, and they were decorated and lit as they had been before.

The construction of Wren's building is complex. The inter-relationship of passages and stairs, the narrowness of apertures through which hoses might have to be passed, the need for stepladders to reach certain critical points, had all to be considered and calculated; the protection of the Cathedral relied on expertise and regular drilling of the air-raid wardens and firefighters.

London is vulnerable to aerial attack. All an enemy aircraft has to do is to follow the line of the river, visible even on a moonless night, leading directly into the heart of London, with the dome of St Paul's a clear silhouette on the skyline. The first bombs fell on London during the night of 24 August 1940, and the first mass attack, concentrated on the Docklands area of the capital, was in the early evening of 7 September. Five days later a high-explosive bomb fell close to the south-west tower, penetrating the road to a depth of nearly 30 feet (9.1 m) and rupturing the gas mains, which caught fire but did not explode. Three days were needed to dig out the device. It was driven to a deserted part of Hackney Marshes and detonated.

Early in the morning of 10 October a direct hit penetrated the roof of the quire, bringing down tons of masonry, shattering the high altar and damaging the reredos. On the worst night of all, 29 December 1940, twenty-eight incendiary bombs fell on or near the Cathedral (fig. 100). The main water supply was hit and failed. The Thames was abnormally low at the time. Tanks, baths and pails of water that had with forethought been installed around the Cathedral

Fig. 101 Watching the skies. After the war, a statue by John W. Mills was set up to London's Fire Brigade. The firemen strove to control the overwhelming flames of the Blitz and subsequent bombings; they succeeded, at a cost.

Fig. 102 St Paul's Watch was formed in the First World War and was re-formed in the Second. These photographs are of the men who guarded the Cathedral from bombs and from fire damage.

Fig. 103 Panoramic view of London made by Cecil Brown from a reconnaissance balloon in 1942 despite the threat of air raids. It shows damage to the roof of the east end and the north transept, and the surrounding devastation.

were now put to good use with stirrup- and hand-pumps. One bomb penetrated the outer shell of the dome, and the lead began to melt. Mercifully, perhaps under its own weight, the bomb fell through on to the Stone Gallery and was extinguished comparatively easily.

On that night the Chapter House on the north side of the Churchyard was destroyed, and so was the whole area around Paternoster Square, which at that time was the centre of newspaper publishing. St Paul's was left standing 'conspicuous and isolated among the ruins', as Dean Matthews later wrote.

Raids on London went on, almost nightly. For just over three months St Paul's remained without further damage. Then, on the night of 16/17 April 1941, it seemed that a concentrated attack was being made on the Cathedral. At about 3 a.m. a heavy bomb went through the roof of the north transept and exploded, bringing down masonry that crashed through the floor into the crypt, shattering the north door and causing the walls of the transept to bulge outwards. Miraculously, the dome remained unmoved (figs 101–3).

The Watch carried on its duties until the end of the war. On 8 May 1945 services – ten in all – were held throughout the day, each of them attended by more than 3,000 people. The concluding service focused on the work of St Paul's Watch, which thereafter disbanded.

Such temporary repairs, or at least coverings-up, as were possible had been put in hand even while the war continued, but once peace came it was time to put the Cathedral to rights. The work was begun by Godfrey Allen, who had so gallantly and effectively commanded the Watch and who rebuilt the Chapter House. It was taken up by Lord Mottistone and Paul Paget, and it was decided not to repair the damaged reredos but to replace it with a white marble high altar sheltered under a Baroque baldacchino designed by Stephen Dykes Bower in collaboration with Allen (figs 104 and 105). This was thought to be far more in keeping with what Wren had intended; his original Communion table, carved by William Samwell, is now in St Dunstan's Chapel at the east end of the north aisle.

The easternmost apse, or Jesus Chapel, was rebuilt from funds raised by the people of Britain, and on 26 November 1958 it was dedicated as the American Memorial (fig. 106). On a pedestal stands a roll of honour inscribed with the names of those Americans serving with the Canadian, British and United States Armed Forces who gave their lives while en route to, or while stationed in, the United Kingdom. It also includes those members of units permanently based in the United Kingdom who made the supreme sacrifice between D Day and VE Day (fig. 107). Three stained-glass windows by Brian Thomas represent Service, Sacrifice and Resurrection. The reredos in the curve of the apse is adorned with eight limewood strips carved in the manner of Grinling Gibbons by George Haslop of Messrs Rattee & Kett of Cambridge; they contain representations of American birds, flowers and fruit. The altar rails, reminiscent of Tijou's work in Wren's day, were provided by Messrs Wainwright & Waring of Mortlake. They show the Burning Bush which appeared to Moses

OPPOSITE:
Fig. 104 The carved and gilded oak baldacchino is surmounted by a gilt figure of Christ, His hand outstretched in blessing.

RIGHT:
Fig. 105 Four square and four round fluted columns and four spiral columns with leaf garlands, all with leafy capitals, support the domed altar canopy.

and the Tablets of the Law on which the Ten Commandments were inscribed, in memory of the many Jewish American servicemen who did not survive the war.

The pulpit was the gift to the Cathedral of Lord Mottistone. He wanted to show that twentieth-century craftsmen could execute work of sufficiently high quality to stand beside that of the seventeenth century.

Wartime damage made it essential for the organ to be rebuilt completely. The work was undertaken by N. P. Mander Ltd in the 1970s and took four years, though the organ-builder contrived that some part of the instrument always stayed in commission and available for the daily services. The console is now above the south choir stalls, with the main instrument

Fig. 106 The American Memorial Chapel at the east end of the Cathedral, immediately behind the High Altar, was dedicated on 26 November 1958.

remaining in two halves on either side of the entrance to the quire, while dome and west-end sections have been added for use when needed. Splendid trumpet stops, displayed *en chamade* (horizontally), have been installed at the west end.

Down in the crypt there has been some fairly extensive rearrangement. The eastern end is the Chapel of St Faith, part of which also serves as the Chapel of the Most Excellent Order of the British Empire (fig. 108). Dedicated in 1960, it has superb furnishings of the period by Lord Mottistone and engraved glass screens by Brian Thomas, with portraits of members of the royal family and landscapes, buildings and animals from many parts of the former British Empire. A fine new organ by William Drake has recently been installed. The small and elegant Knights Bachelor Chapel in the south-east corner of the crypt was dedicated in 2008 in the presence of HM The Queen and HRH The Duke of Edinburgh in celebration of the centenary of the Imperial Society of Knights Bachelor.

Around the Duke of Wellington's sarcophagus have been arranged large tablets with the names of the Field Marshals of the Second World War. It is a sombre place, set apart, a long-term reminder of courage, determination and loss. Not far away is a large slate tablet, carved by David Kindersley, to the memory of the 255 men who lost their lives in the Falklands Campaign of 1982 in the South Atlantic.

Over the past twenty-five years the Chapter, through the sensitive but bold designs of Surveyor Martin Stancliffe, have transformed work and worship in St Paul's. In 1999 a new sanctuary was created under the dome, thus bringing the place of celebration right into the congregation. St Dunstan's Chapel, at the west end of the north aisle, is set aside for private prayer and has become a place where visitors can stop and be still for a moment and capture something of the meaning of a living faith. Holman Hunt's famous *Light of the World* now stands as an altarpiece in the centre of the Middlesex Chapel, another quiet reflective space. The newly lighted crypt provides amenities and refreshments for visitors beside an excellent bookshop with well-chosen souvenirs. The building and its history are interpreted by a video display called Oculus.

A steady round of worship is kept up, with four services daily and a fifth on Sundays. Both the 1662 Book of Common Prayer and the revised Book of Common Worship are in use. Special services are held for national occasions of mourning, such as the bombing of the Twin Towers in New York in 2001 and the London Transport bombings of 7 July 2005, and also celebration, such as Queen Elizabeth the Queen Mother's hundredth birthday in 2000 and Her Majesty Queen Elizabeth II's eightieth birthday in 2006. Services are also held for major charities,

Fig. 107 'Defending Freedom from the Fierce Assault of Tyranny': lettering on the beautifully illuminated American Roll of Honour.

schools, livery companies, professional bodies, regiments and some orders of chivalry. The service held on the fourth Thursday in November for Thanksgiving Day is truly appreciated by the American community in England. The long-standing service for Sons of the Clergy raises funds for dependants of clergy in times of financial necessity or distress.

The great festivals of the Christian year – Christmas, Easter and Pentecost – are occasions for particular rejoicing. Between Christmas and Epiphany a Christmas tree stands under the portico, with two more inside, under the dome. There is also a crib, carved by the cathedral's own sculptors (Tony Webb and Hannah Hartwell), with the Christ Child in the manger, surrounded by Mary, Joseph, the ox and the ass, and the shepherds. Processional services of music and readings for Advent, Christmas, Epiphany, Passiontide and Whitsuntide make dramatic liturgical use of the entire body of the building and its remarkable acoustic.

Since St Paul's has no parish, it has only a small regular congregation; perhaps three-quarters of those attending services are visitors. To some extent the anonymity of the congregations lays a duty of primary evangelism on the clergy. There is always someone in the Cathedral ready to give pastoral care – to say prayers with or for those in need, to hear confession, to give practical advice. Although throngs pass in and out of the great Cathedral, the individual is neither forgotten nor ignored. At the same time, those who have responsibility for St Paul's strive to make sure that all who enter have space to find their own thoughts.

The daily work of the Cathedral receives much support from the Friends of St Paul's Cathedral. This is a body of men and women, formed in 1953 and now 2,500 strong, who believe in the special significance of St Paul's. Most are content simply to pay a modest subscription, but some 150 who are able, and have time to give, share in the duties – welcoming visitors, guiding them, lecturing to schoolchildren and other passing groups, and helping to make visitors feel at home in the vast building. The Duchess of Gloucester is Patron of the Friends and regularly attends their annual service.

Almost inevitably, it has been necessary to charge tourist visitors, though not those attending services or Friends, for admission to St Paul's. In 1868 the endowments of the Cathedral passed to the Ecclesiastical Commissioners, and the Chapter are today solely responsible for the costs of maintaining the Cathedral and its mission. Substantial donations made possible the cleaning of the whole exterior and interior of the Cathedral, a major undertaking which was completed in time for the 300th anniversary of Wren's building, marked in 2011 with a service of thanksgiving attended by the Queen and Duke of Edinburgh and the whole cathedral family of clergy, staff and volunteers.

Next to the services and the maintenance of the building, the Cathedral's most important responsibility is for education. The choir of men and boys has been an essential part of the services since earliest times (fig. 112), and choirboys need teaching. St Paul's Cathedral School lies to the south-east of the Cathedral and now provides for the choristers and 200 day pupils,

both boys and girls, aged four to thirteen; the tower of the bombed church of St Augustine Watling Street incorporated at the south-west corner is a perfect foil to school and Cathedral.

The school is only a part of the Cathedral's educational work. The Education Department, with a fully paid staff and many volunteers, hosts a quarter of a million schoolchildren each year for lessons on faith, ministry and history in the Education Centre in the crypt, and visits to highlights upstairs. The St Paul's Institute hosts regular seminars that strive to reach across the boundaries of professional life, and to focus on Christian spirituality and theology and on the ethics of the workplace and capitalism.

The Cathedral Chapter is anxious to encourage the placing of works of art in and around

Fig. 109 Henry Moore's *Mother and Child* was specially created for St Paul's and is on permanent loan from the Henry Moore Foundation.

Fig. 110 *Mother and Child* by Josefina de Vasconcellos, a work in *Terrosa Ferrata* stone. It was presented to the Cathedral in 1957 by Bernard Sunley.

the building. In 1999 a low, free-standing, circular memorial, carved by Richard Kindersley, was set up in the Churchyard outside the north transept, celebrating the steadfastness of the people of London during the bombing of the Second World War. Within the Cathedral, an exquisite silver hanging pyx by Rod Kelly has been installed in St Dunstan's Chapel, and there are two twentieth-century works by Josefina de Vasconcellos and Henry Moore (figs 109 and 110). In 2004 the Churchill Memorial Gates were installed, separating the OBE Chapel and other public areas of the crypt from Nelson's and Wellington's tombs as part of a complete transformation of the crypt by Martin Stancliffe. The gates were created by James Horrobin and his team to commemorate the concern shown by Churchill for the safety of St Paul's. Each

morning on waking, the Prime Minister's first enquiry was, 'Is the dome still safe?' The screen was dedicated, on 30 November 2004, the 130th anniversary of Churchill's birth.

The aspect of the southern approach to St Paul's was altered fundamentally by the opening of the Millennium Bridge, linking the two banks of the Thames. Sweeping flights of steps smooth the path up and down, and on the summit, close to the Cathedral, stands a memorial to the London Fire Brigade, which so valiantly defended the capital. To the north of St Paul's, Lord Holford's bleak laying out of devastated Paternoster Square has been replaced by a gentler arrangement. On its southern side Wren's Temple Bar gives access to the Square. Built after 1666 but removed as a traffic obstruction in 1878 to Hertfordshire, it was at last restored to the City on 10 November 2004. A coach park has been replaced with a new Jubilee Gardens.

In October 2011 anti-capitalist protesters pitched a tent city outside St Paul's. Even if by coincidence, the Cathedral became an international symbol of the challenges raised by the

Fig. 111 A special service to mark the tenth anniversary of ALMA, the link between Anglican churches in Angola, London and Mozambique, filled the Cathedral in 2008. The three partner Bishops, Dinis Sengulane, André Soares and Mark Van Koevering, and the Reverend Helen Van Koevering joined Bishops Richard Chartres and Michael Colclough.

Fig. 112 St Paul's choristers wear medals in recognition of the generosity of benefactors in supporting the maintenance of the Choir.

OVERLEAF:
Fig. 113 The Queen and other members of the royal family attended a thanksgiving service at St Paul's Cathedral to mark the Diamond Jubilee.

protest. Concerns over how to respond placed terrible pressure on the Chapter and the Cathedral's staff, culminating in the first closure of the building since the Second World War, and the resignations of the Dean and Canon Chancellor. Although a challenging chapter in the Cathedral's long history, these events have inspired productive reflection and debate about St Paul's role in the diocese, the nation and the world.

The Queen's Diamond Jubilee, commemorating the sixtieth year of Her Majesty's reign, was celebrated over three days in 2012. On Sunday 3 June Her Majesty, accompanied by Prince Philip, Duke of Edinburgh, and the royal family, boarded a royal barge decorated like those painted by Canaletto and, followed by a fleet of over a thousand smaller vessels, sailed down the Thames from Battersea to Tower Bridge. The celebrations culminated on 5 June in a service of thanksgiving at St Paul's Cathedral in the heart of London, her capital; the service gave thanks for the Commonwealth, other faiths and the charities of which she is patron.

Fig. 114 Accompanied by Prince Charles, Prince of Wales, Prince William, Duke of Cambridge, Camilla, Duchess of Cornwall, Catherine, Duchess of Cambridge and Prince Harry, the Queen processed through the nave following the service of thanksgiving.

Fig. 115 The Queen leaves St Paul's Cathedral, following a service to commemorate the Diamond Jubilee, with the Dean of St Paul's, the Very Reverend Dr David Ison (left) and the Right Reverend Michael Colclough, Canon Pastor (right).

Fig. 116 The royal barge, *the Spirit of Chartwell*, sailed east along the River Thames as part of the Diamond Jubilee pageant. Along the river, paths, rooftops and bridges were crowded with well-wishers.

INDEX

BIBLIOGRAPHY

London

Black, J. 2009. *London: A History.* Lancaster, Carnegie

Hibbert, C. 1980. *London: The Biography of a City.* Harmondsworth, Penguin

Levine, J. M. 1999. *Ancients and Moderns: Baroque Culture in Restoration England.* New Haven, CT, Yale University Press

Porter, R. 1994. *London: A Social History.* London, Hamish Hamilton

Reddaway, T. 1940. *The Rebuilding of London after the Great Fire.* London, Jonathan Cape

Saunders, A. 1984. *The Art and Architecture of London: An Illustrated Guide.* Oxford, Phaidon

St Paul's Cathedral and Wren

Burman, P. 1987. *St Paul's Cathedral.* London, Bell & Hyman

Campbell, J. W. P. 2007. *Building St Paul's.* London, Thames & Hudson

Downes, K. 1998. *St Paul's and its Architecture: A Tercentenary Lecture.* York, Redhedge

Geraghty, A. 2007. *The Architectural Drawings of Sir Christopher Wren at All Souls College, Oxford: A Complete Catalogue.* Aldershot, Lund Humphries

Gerbino, A. and S. Johnston. 2009. *Compass and Rule: Architecture as Mathematical Practice.* New Haven, CT, Yale University Press

Jardine, L. 1999. *Ingenious Pursuits: Building the Scientific Revolution.* London, Little, Brown & Co.

Jardine, L. 2002. *On a Grander Scale: The Outstanding Career of Sir Christopher Wren.* London, Harper Collins

Keene D., A. Burns and A. Saint (editors). 2004. *St Paul's: the Cathedral Church of London, 604–2004.* New Haven, CT, Yale University Press

Lang, J. 1956. *Rebuilding St Paul's after the Great Fire of London.* London, Oxford University Press

Morrissey, M. 2011. *Politics and the Paul's Cross Sermons, 1558–1642.* Oxford, Oxford University Press

Rousseau, M.-H. 2011. *Saving the Souls of Medieval London: Perpetual Chantries at St. Paul's Cathedral, c.1200–1548.* Farnham, Ashgate

Schofield, J. 2011. *St Paul's Cathedral Before Wren.* Swindon, English Heritage

Wren Society. 20 vols. 1924–1943. Oxford, Oxford University Press for the Wren Society

Author's Acknowledgements

I am grateful to the Chapter of St Paul's for encouraging me in the preparation of my book, and to Scala for their handsome production. I give Peter McCullough thanks for his guidance, in particular with the recent history of the Cathedral. Joseph Wisdom, the Cathedral Librarian, gave support beyond the call of duty as well as compiling the bibliography. John Schofield, Cathedral Archaeologist, gave heartening advice. Jeremy Smith at London Metropolitan Archive helped with enthusiasm, as did Linda Fisher in Oxford. Margaret Mander FSA generously allowed the reproduction of her father's treasured drawing by Cecil Brown of bomb damage. Christopher MacLehose gave invaluable advice. My husband, son, daughter-in-law and two grandsons were unfailingly encouraging.

This edition © 2012 Scala Publishers Ltd
Text © 2012 Ann Saunders
Photography © 2012 St Paul's Cathedral, by Angelo Hornak, except for those listed opposite

First published in 2012 by
Scala Publishers Ltd
Northburgh House
10 Northburgh St
London EC1V 0AT
Telephone: +44 (0) 20 7490 9900
www.scalapublishers.com

in association with St Paul's Cathedral

Hardback ISBN: 978-1-85759-802-5
Paperback ISBN: 978-1-85759-807-0

Project editor: Esme West
Copy editor: Matthew Taylor
Designer: Nigel Soper
Printed and bound in Singapore

10 9 8 7 6 5 4 3 2 1

INSIDE COVER:
The Thames and the City of London from the Terrace of Somerset House by Antonio Canaletto.